W9-AOD-067

King Saul's Asking

INTERFACES

Series Editor: Barbara Green, O.P.

King Saul's Asking

Barbara Green, O.P.

A Michael Glazier Book

LITURGICAL PRESS

Collegeville, Minnesota

www.litpress.org

222.43092
Grk

A Michael Glazier Book published by the Liturgical Press.

Cover design by Ann Blattner. Watercolor by Ethel Boyle.

The Scripture quotations, unless otherwise indicated, are from the New Revised Standard Version Bible © 1989 by the Division of Christian Education of the National Council of Churches of Christ in the U.S.A. Used by permission. All rights reserved.

© 2003 by The Order of Saint Benedict, Collegeville, Minnesota. All rights reserved. No part of this book may be reproduced in any form or by any means, electronic or mechanical, including photocopying, recording, taping, or any retrieval system, without the written permission of the Liturgical Press, Collegeville, Minnesota 56321. Printed in the United States of America.

1	2	3	4	5	6	7	8	9

Library of Congress Cataloging-in-Publication Data

Green, Barbara, 1946–
 King Saul's asking / Barbara Green.
  p. cm. — (Interfaces)
 "A Michael Glazier book."
 Includes bibliographical references.
 ISBN 0-8146-5109-7 (alk. paper)
  1. Saul, King of Israel. 2. Bible. O.T. Samuel—Criticism, interpretation, etc.
 I. Title. II. Interfaces (Collegeville, Minn.)

BS580.S3 G74 2003
222'.43092—dc21
                                                                2002073062

DEDICATION

In the years just after Vatican II leadership in religious communities, never easy, became additionally challenging. The culture was changing rapidly, unexpectedly. Gifts and skills shaped over a lifetime, which had sustained individuals, groups, and relationships, were no longer useful or appreciated. New skills had yet to be identified and honed. A woman in my Dominican community was elected to major congregational leadership at this time (the mid-1960s). She was tall, genial, easygoing in many ways, well-beloved by her friends. And yet those qualities, tempered in her by others theretofore more hidden—a certain rigidity, even scrupulosity—made the years of her leadership difficult for her, her friends, her sisters. I recall a number of small encounters with her—they seemed large at the time—and certain ones related by my friends. In retrospect, of course, issues were larger and more complex than we judged them to be, and failings were not simply personal but often structural. But in any case we survived, and this woman, Sister M. George deLorimier, resumed her more collegial life among her sisters in the years after her term of office ended. Her gentle, humorous, and generous qualities re-emerged. She carried virtually no rancor from the years when she had been Mother General, and any suffering seemed to increase her compassion. She became to me and others a wonderful old/new friend who knew many wise things. This volume of INTERFACES is about a tall man, unexpectedly asked to lead his community at a time of great change and uncertainty. He does not do very well, for reasons we will explore together in this book. As I have come to know this biblical character from my several years spent on "Saul projects," Sister George has been much and often on my mind. After her death I learned that she had provided for me a small bequest to assist my life of prayer and study. That thoughtful gift has assisted this project in several ways. Since it tells a story of "strugglous" leadership, but one where graces do not lack, this book is dedicated to the memory of Sister M.George de Lorimier, O.P. I am also most grateful to the generosity of Richard Cassidy for his cheerful help and practical support and to Bula Maddison who has assisted me on every page with her skill and gentleness.

CONTENTS

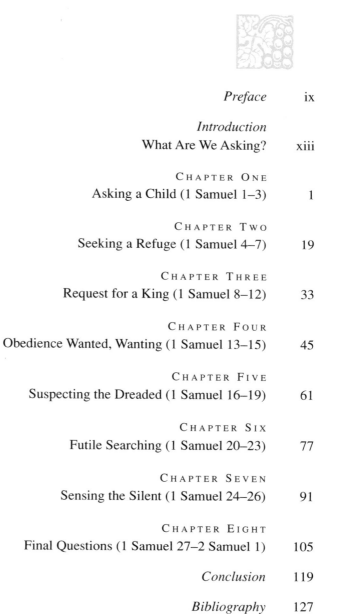

PREFACE

The book you hold in your hand is one of six volumes in a new set. This series, called INTERFACES, is a curriculum and scholarly adventure, a creative opportunity in teaching and learning, presented at this moment in the long story of how the Bible has been studied, interpreted, and appropriated.

The INTERFACES project was prompted by a number of experiences that you, perhaps, share. When I first taught undergraduates the college had just received a substantial grant from the National Endowment for the Humanities, and one of the recurring courses designed within the grant was called Great Figures in Pursuit of Excellence. Three courses would be taught, each centering on a figure from some academic discipline or other, with a common seminar section to provide occasion for some integration. Some triads were more successful than others, as you might imagine. But the opportunity to concentrate on a single individual—whether historical or literary—to team teach, to make links to another pair of figures, and to learn new things about other disciplines was stimulating and fun for all involved. A second experience that gave rise to the present series came at the same time, connected also with undergraduates. It was my frequent experience to have Roman Catholic students feel quite put out about taking "more" biblical studies since, as they confidently affirmed, they had already been there many times and done it all. That was, of course, not true; as we well know, there is always more to learn. And often those who felt most informed were the least likely to take on new information when offered it.

A stimulus as primary as my experience with students was the familiarity of listening to friends and colleagues at professional meetings talking about the research that excites us most. I often wondered: Do her undergraduate students know about this? Or how does he bring these ideas— clearly so energizing to him—into the college classroom? Perhaps some of us have felt bored with classes that seem wholly unrelated to research, that rehash the same familiar material repeatedly. Hence the idea for this series of books to bring to the fore and combine some of our research interest with our teaching and learning. Accordingly, this series is not so much about creating texts *for* student audiences, but rather about *sharing* our scholarly passions with them. Because these volumes are intended each as a piece of original scholarship they are geared to be stimulating to both students and established scholars, perhaps resulting in some fruitful collaborative learning adventures.

The series also developed from a widely-shared sense that all academic fields are expanding and exploding, and that to contemplate "covering" even a testament (let alone the whole Bible or Western monotheistic religions) needs to be abandoned in favor of something with greater depth. At the same time the links between our fields are becoming increasingly obvious as well, and we glimpse exciting possibilities for ways of working that will draw together academic realms that once seemed separate. Finally, the spark of enthusiasm that almost always ignites when I mention to colleagues and students the idea of single figures in combination—interfacing—encourages me that this is an idea worth trying.

And so with the leadership and help of Liturgical Press Academic Editor Linda Maloney, as well as with the encouragement and support of Managing Editor Mark Twomey, the series has begun to take shape.

Each volume in the INTERFACES series focuses clearly on a biblical character (or perhaps a pair of them). The characters are in some cases powerful (King Saul, Pontius Pilate) and familiar (John the Baptist, Joseph) though in other cases they will strike many as minor and little-known (the Cannibal Mothers, Herodias). In any case, each of them has been chosen to open up a set of worlds for consideration. The named (or unnamed) character interfaces with his or her historical-cultural world and its many issues, with other characters from biblical literature; each character has drawn forth the creativity of the author, who has taken on the challenge of engaging many readers. The books are specifically designed for college students (though we think suitable for some graduate work as well), planned to provide young adults with relevant information and at a level of critical sophistication that matches the rest of the undergraduate curriculum. In fact, the expectation is that what students are learning in other classes on historiography, literary theory, and cultural anthropology will find an echo in these books, each of which is explicit about at least two relevant methodologies. It is surely the case that biblical studies is in a methodology-conscious moment, and the INTERFACES series embraces it enthusiastically. Our hope is for students (and teachers) to continue to see the relationship between their best questions and their most valuable insights, between how they approach texts and what they find there. The volumes go well beyond familiar paraphrase of narratives to ask questions that are relevant in our era. At the same time the series authors have each dealt with the notion of the Bible as Scripture in a way that is comfortable for them. None of the books is preachy or hortatory, and yet the self-implicating aspects of working with the revelatory text are handled frankly. The assumption is, again, that college can be a good time for students to rethink their beliefs and assumptions, and they need to do so in good company.

The INTERFACES volumes are not substitutes for the Bible. In every case they are to be read with the text. Quoting has been kept to a minimum for that very reason. The volumes, when used in a classroom setting, are accompanied by a companion volume, *From Earth's Creation to John's Revelation: The INTERFACES Biblical Storyline Companion,* which provides a quick, straightforward overview of the whole storyline into which the characters under special study fit. Web links will also be available through the Liturgical Press website: www.litpress.org.

The series challenge—for publisher, writers, teachers, and students— is to combine the volumes creatively, to "interface" them well so that the vast potential of the biblical text continues to unfold for all of us. The first six volumes: in Old Testament/Hebrew Bible featuring Saul, the Cannibal Mothers, and Joseph; in New Testament focusing on John the Baptist, Herodias, and Pontius Pilate, offer a foretaste of other volumes currently in preparation. It has been a pleasure, and a richly informative privilege, to work with the authors of these first volumes as well as the series consultants: Carleen Mandolfo for Hebrew Bible and Catherine Murphy for New Testament. It is the hope of all of us that you will find the series useful and stimulating for your own teaching and learning.

Barbara Green, O.P.
INTERFACES Series Editor
June 29, 2002
Berkeley, California

INTRODUCTION
What Are We Asking?

Have you ever wanted something very badly, asked for it insistently until you received it, but then reappraised your desire, once it was fulfilled? Or have you ever been certain that you did *not* want something, though others told you that you did or ought to wish it, but then struggle to hang onto it once it began to slip from your fingers? If either of those experiences has been yours, then you will find yourself at home in the story of King Saul, for those two dynamics shape the story like tides at the beach. Certain characters in Saul's story ask urgently for a king, feel they must have one as others do, but then some come to regret the candidate they get. And the man who is asked to be king tries in a number of ways, though ineffectually, to avoid the role. But when he is fired from his job early in his career, he refuses to vacate and dies with the crown still on his head, having paid heavily—and cost others mightily—for the role he thought he did not want.

How will *we* read this story, which unfolds in the biblical book of 1 Samuel? The series Foreword lays out some of the features you may expect. Read it if you have not already done so. And the background that accompanies the INTERFACES volumes reviews where this story fits the biblical storyline. Saul's story comes early in the period of biblical Israel, which is to say it is set as a story of origins or foundations. The community known as Israel (and later as the Jewish people) had been called into a relationship with God in the persons of Abraham and Sarah, whose descendants had refugeed to Egypt for food, languished in slavery there, escaped unexpectedly, and then wandered in the wilderness before returning to the land called Canaan. Since resettling they have had troubles with their neighbors, and Israel's own clearest lack is stable leadership. As you can see from the background information and as you will read shortly, monarchy with its apparent assumption of dynastic succession appeared to be an improvement over the *ad hoc* sort of troubleshooting leaders who preceded the asking of Saul to be king.

But a story's setting is not necessarily the same as the circumstances of its production, which we know if we stop to think about it, and an old tale surely seems far from our own time. The story purports to tell of events taking place in the late 1100s B.C.E., but I stipulate here (without argument) that the story was produced (probably from older tales) much later, in the sixth century, to address concerns of an Israelite community in exile. If King David's traditional date is 1000, Saul's narrative setting will be the time just preceding that. In the early sixth century much of the community went into exile to Babylon with the last king; but it is also clear that the monarchy ends definitively before the end of the 500s. Saul's story in 1 Samuel comes early in the long narrative of the Israelites that stretches from Deuteronomy through 2 Kings (comprising what biblical scholars are mostly content to call the Deuteronomistic History).[1] My position, stipulated rather than argued here, is that the historical circumstances we need to ponder most attentively are those of the production of the story, the sixth rather than the eleventh century. That old stories can be vitally helpful for later readers is also something with which we are familiar, many differences notwithstanding. But if we are to get at what the story offers us we need to read skillfully. Reading well, with appropriate strategies and critical consciousness of our own moves, is the most important challenge we can set ourselves.

Once I have decided for us that Saul's tale in 1 Samuel reads best as an exile story, what other suggestions about interpretation follow for the book and its readers? What else will we be asking to get at the communication of this text? Though I have been a professional biblical scholar for more than thirty years, the theorist who has taught me the most has only crossed my path recently—and our encounter did not take place in the field of Old Testament studies! Russian philosopher, literary critic and anthropologist Mikhail Bakhtin (1895–1975) was a man who lived his life under Soviet domination. Though he has become widely read (at least in scholarly circles!), such popularity would have left him bemused, I think. That he is the teacher from whom I have learned best how to read the biblical text would, I know, be a surprise, but not an unpleasant one, I trust. His ways of reading are brilliant and provocative. Being widely appropriated across disciplines, his ideas do not lack people to praise and critique them as valuable (or not) in various fields. We will not go deeply into Bakhtin's thought, though you may do so if your interest becomes piqued.[2] From the many

---

[1] A recent work on this hypothesis and text can be approached via Antony F. Campbell and Mark A. O'Brien, *Unfolding the Deuteronomistic History: Origins, Upgrades, Present Text* (Minneapolis: Fortress, 2000).

[2] See Barbara Green, *Mikhail Bakhtin and Biblical Scholarship: An Introduction* (Atlanta: Society of Biblical Literature Press, 2000) chs. 1 and 2.

things he says we will borrow three large concepts for our use and shape them into methodological tools that will be at home in Old Testament studies, though you will have encountered them in other parts of the curriculum as well. Those three concepts are *genre,* varieties of *discourse,* and *answerability.* Let me explain each briefly, with enough detail to suggest our way forward but without overwhelming the reading we need to do.

Genre is most fundamentally for Bakhtin a mode of creativity, a shape that thinking tends to take. As a strategy for crafting an utterance it utilizes the social baggage our language bears while it works at envisioning. Genres organize our thought and speech somewhat as grammar does, provide some stability for utterances—whether spoken language or literature. Bakhtin observes: "Each separate utterance is individual, of course, but each sphere in which language is used develops its own *relatively stable types* of these utterances. These we may call *speech genres.*"[3]

We may also understand what Bakhtin is suggesting by noting what he says genres are not. Genre is not to be confused with a collection of devices. That is, scrutiny and classification of morphological elements has little to do with genre and is a fundamentally misleading way to approach it. Genre is sometimes equated with what is called "form" in biblical studies, and there is indeed a similarity. Consider the notion of sandals. Suppose you decide that you wish to own a pair, for some project that lies ahead in your life—perhaps a week at the beach. You can start by looking around at the footwear of everyone within your current range: who is wearing sandals? What *is* a sandal? And you could make a list of formal features, criteria that "your sandal" must satisfy. You may have to adjudicate claims: is a Birkenstock inevitably a member of the formal family sandal? Can sandals have laces? What about clogs or other shoes with an open heel? And if you went into a shoestore, or onto the Internet, you could consume a great deal of time trying to construct a template for the concept you are talking about. You might even miss your week at the beach—or decide you are too exhausted to go! But suppose, on the other hand, you began not with the abstract notion of sandalness but with your own feet and your own vacation plans; as you begin to work out your specific hopes and think about your footwear needs you may ask some of the same questions just unfolded above. But you will not be interested in the abstraction, or care about a neat and complete chart. You will be weighing the actual circumstances of walking in the sand with sandals, slipping them off as you enter

---

[3] Bakhtin wrote in many places about genre. A late essay that recapitulates much of his earlier thought is "The Problem of Speech Genres," in his *Speech Genres and Other Late Essays,* edited by Caryl Emerson and Michael Holquist, translated by Vern W. McGee (Austin: University of Texas Press, 1986) 60 (emphasis in original).

the house, propping them on comfortable furniture as you relax to read, and so forth.

How does genre advance our study of Saul, you may be asking. Though the story of the first king may be classified at the macro-level as a narrative, I will try to ensure that we read it as a riddle. Though I will explain more fully in Chapter Two, let me indicate here that our riddle is one of a particular type of imagery, common in the Old Testament, called a *mashal:* one thing is suggested to be like (and unlike) another. A riddle is a genre; riddles can be classified into as many sub-forms as shoes can: elephant jokes, shaggy dog stories, puns, and so forth. The story of Saul, and indeed the character himself, is—or may be responsibly read as—the long and subtle answer to the question: When the exile community prepares to return to Judea from Babylon, once it is possible to do so (after 539 or so), shall the people return under the leadership of kings or not? In retrospect we can see that the answer is pretty clear: without kings. How to make so basic a change? It cannot have been an obvious or easy shift at the time, and there is evidence to suggest that a royal figure may well have led the return but then been bypassed somehow. In any case he did not survive and was not replaced. There are many reasons to have stayed with monarchic leadership that will be reviewed below when appropriate. But the answer, made clear in and by the story of Saul as he embodies the monarchic experience of Israel, shouts "no more kings!" However, we cannot hear the answer until we can ask the question, and we will not be able to ask the riddle's question until we recognize the genre we are dealing with. We have all watched a child take a joke "seriously" and know intuitively what kind of category mistake it is. Attending with some care to the genre of riddle may help us read our story well, as appraising footgear works best with actual needs in mind.

A second area of study where Bakhtin observed literature most carefully can be called *varieties of discourse,* what biblical scholar Carol Newsom calls "the complex voicing of speech."[4] This phenomenon simply calls attention to how a reader is given information: by a narrator, via a reverie or soliloquy, as characters talk about each other, and so forth. Bakhtin talks about this set of language characteristics intermittently as he writes: sometimes with greater stress on and interest in the linguistic features and sometimes drawing more attention to the social dimension. Occasionally he was interested more in theme (or content), but other times in the manner of representation—now in the conventional while later perhaps in the idiosyncratic—but never wholly separating the diverse pairs that can so easily

---

[4] Carol A. Newsom has a short and good introduction: "Bakhtin," in A.K.M. Adam, ed., *Handbook of Postmodern Biblical Interpretation* (St. Louis: Chalice Press, 2000) 20–27.

be dichotomized in theory. Language on the hoof (whether "live" or literary) is always attending to a variety of tasks with myriad relationalities already established and at work. The opposite of these Bakhtinian assumptions is anything simplex, wholly or adequately reducible to a formula or a chart, any positivistic appropriation, the applying of "messages" from one situation to another (unfortunately popular within various sorts of biblical study), the temptation to crystallize "the meaning" of an utterance, and so forth. Bakhtin's sense of language calls into question the practices and results of such procedures (which he names and with which he argues in his own early-twentieth-century Russian context rather than in situations more familiar and useful to us now). For him the choices are not on a crude spectrum forcing us into either positivistic certainty or chaotic nihilism. Rather, as each of us participates in the complexity of the voicing, selecting some aspects and bypassing others, attending to certain things while disregarding others, our construction of meaning will be fresh and distinctive, particular though again communal as well; not in any sense isolated from the web in which we are flailing, we are nonetheless not reproducing the choices of anyone else.[5]

If you think about literature (at least classical and most modern), the text is composed of what characters say or what the narrator says. I offer here for our quick common consideration a scene where parents are trying to extract information from offspring in front of some other authority—perhaps school personnel. How does each parent address the son or daughter, using what address, what tone, what language? Are questions helpful, assertions of what must be the case, angry accusations? Do the parents draw in the other authority, perhaps by summarizing what the interrogated person has just said? If so, is the summary made fairly or not? What kind of language attends the discussion: legal, familial, relational, or adversarial? What is the effect when the accusations of others, not present in the room, are brought forth? Do some of the phrases of the parents make the son or daughter cringe? Why? As you fill out this scenario with rich detail, which I hope you will do, weigh the differences among the various portions of the information that emerge. If we listen attentively we can pick up on many things beyond what is plainly said.

But how can such an imagined scene help us know how to listen as we read biblical text? What does that tell us to watch for in our story of Saul?

---

[5] Bakhtin's best discussions of language are in his work on Dostoevsky, *Problems of Dostoevsky's Poetics*, edited and translated by Caryl Emerson (Minneapolis: University of Minnesota Press, 1984) ch. 5, and in his more theoretical discussion authored with V. N. Voloshinov, *Marxism and the Philosophy of Language*, translated by Ladislav Matejka and I. R. Titunik (Cambridge, Mass.: Harvard University Press, 1973) part III, chs. 1–3.

Though I will make more specific and additional suggestions below, we can begin to notice who talks, how they talk, whether they engage others directly or obliquely; we can note whose heads we get to enter and how language works there. We can mine speech for subtle currents of viewpoint or ideology, perhaps picking up on things of which the characters and narrator betray little consciousness. We can notice how common the speech of friends is, or what differences may attend class or gender, though everyone is speaking "the same" tongue. And we will watch how uneven the narrator is with discourse. In other contexts you may have learned that a narrator is reliable, omniscient, and objective. Bakhtin's observations expose that set of assumptions as inadequate and misleading. Feminist literary critic Alice Bach urges us to "name" a narrator, by which she means characterize that voice in relation to the characters managed.[6] The "Saul narrator," we shall see, has many ways to tell us the story we are reading, and the variety of options challenges our readerly ingenuity. We will see, for example, that we are rather often privy to Saul's private conversation, so that we know what he aims for and so often misses. Conversely, we rarely have any inside view of David, so he is presented to us as enigmatic, cards-held-to-his-chest, much more difficult to appraise. How the narrator handles God is crucial for our reading. The depiction of God in the Bible is rich, multiform, and contradictory. No single portrait has got it just right, and it is important that we not literalize the character God into a, into *the* actual deity. The way God is brought into language in this narrative will tell us no small amount about how the deity is envisioned, is desired to be, at the time of the story's narration. But it is important that we not mistake the particularities of divine characterization for literal images of God.

Bakhtin's third concept on which we can draw he called *answerability*. That notion brings us into the realm of the ethical and moral and to the field of biblical spirituality. Most succinctly, answerability is the lifework of becoming a self. A cluster of comments by two Bakhtin scholars ramifies the point a bit:

> Each of us occupies a unique time and place in life, an existence that is conceived not as a passive state but as an activity, an event. I calibrate the time and place of my own position, which is always shifting, in the existence of other human beings and the natural world by means of the values that I articulate in deeds. Ethics is not abstract principles but the pattern of actual deeds I perform in the event that is my life.

---

[6] Alice Bach, *Women, Seduction, and Betrayal in Biblical Narrative* (Cambridge: Cambridge University Press, 1997) ch. 2.

My self is that through which such performance answers other selves
and the world from the unique place and time I occupy in existence.[7]

All authorship—"live" or literary—involves answerability. We may
think of a literary artist drawing a king, or we ponder how a human being
struggles to be a king; we reflect upon the intensive relatedness between
God and creatures, or about ourselves working to make a go of a relationship that seems important. All of these efforts are authorings and all
involve answerability. Bakhtin has two terms for the refusal to live answerably, and he supplements them with other contraries as well. First, his
"pretender" seeks to avoid the project of selfhood, primarily by living according to others' norms or by hiding within a role that allows for representative or ritualistic living, where "perks" of the role are assimilated to
one's own sense of self; he or she might live like a character in a novel. We
might think of other likelier places than novels where this particular temptation lies—Hollywood, Madison Avenue, Wall Street, or some more local
address—but in any case some place where we absorb certain reigning
norms of our own subcultures, handing over to that authority decisions that
need to be made by the self; pretending, in this sense, can also mean over-
rating the self one sees in the mirror. Bakhtin's second name for refusing
answerability is to live with an "alibi in Being"; this means for Bakhtin
to live nowhere, that is, elsewhere from where in fact one is situated.
Bakhtin's alibi-in-Being can be clarified as follows, according to his translator Liapunov: "I cannot be relieved of answerability for the commission
of an act by an *alibi,* that is, by claiming to have been *elsewhere* than at the
place of commission."[8]

This concept is perhaps less strange to us than genre and discourse,
since you are likely by this time in your lives to have made conscious
choices, perhaps a series of them, where you have committed yourself to a
pathway that seems intrinsically part of your integrity. The difficulty
comes in doing the answerable deed, maintaining it as a life project, and
seeing the same dynamic in art as well as in life. Though Bakhtin seems to
have remained a deeply-committed believer in God, his writings urge that
we not utterly ground our actual choices in rules and abstract postulates,

[7] For the best secondary study on this concept see Katerina Clark and Michael Holquist,
Mikhail Bakhtin (Cambridge, Mass.: Harvard University Press, 1984); this quotation is on
p. 64 and developed in ch. 3 more generally.

[8] Bakhtin discussed this concept in several places, perhaps most accessibly in his
Toward a Philosophy of the Act, edited by Vadim Liapunov and Michael Holquist, translated
by Vadim Liapunov (Austin: University of Texas Press, 1993). Liapunov adds some clarifying notes: see his n. 111 on p. 95.

even crucial ones. Our selfhood project—which obviously involves our relations with all our others, God included—must be worked out as we go, not chaotically or nihilistically, not in denial of norms and relationships, and surely not by making them our alibi or the place from which we can pretend.

Though I will suggest that Saul's major characteristic is his refusal of responsibility, an incapacity for answerability, his being drawn with that trait is not an end in itself. If I am right about the story of Saul propounding a riddle that its original exilic audience must claim and read, the story also offers us, its much later readers, a mirror as well as a riddle. As we engage the story of this very human character as he struggles with so many difficulties—even those he invites himself—to the degree that we negotiate his story and allow it to pose to us some of its best questions we can open up the possibility of some transformation in ourselves. Of course almost anything that we let into our lives changes us at least infinitesimally, but depending on our assumptions when we interpret this story we can deepen our self-knowledge and move more consciously in one direction or another. One name for such a process is spirituality.

Sandra Schneiders has written lucidly and compellingly about biblical spirituality, which she characterizes most foundationally as concerned with specifically religious and transformative experience. It assists the integration of the reader or reading community toward what is perceived to be of ultimate value. For Christians that is the triune God revealed in Jesus and appropriated through a living of the paschal mystery in the context of the church community through the gift of the Holy Spirit.[9] I will not presume to describe what *you* want to do when reading, but I will suggest what motivates me and the most vitally engaged circles within which I read. One of the most wonderful capacities of our humanity is our participation in the self-disclosure of God, which includes constitutively discerning it from within our experience. The Bible is a privileged place for such an encounter, not the only one, but a very rich site. How to read biblical texts transformatively, so that they draw us ever more deeply into the mystery of being human in relationship with God, becomes the key question. The moves we can and must make to participate in such an encounter will both draw deeply on the many riches of the tradition of which we are a part and also be compatible with the particular worlds in which we currently live. That is, responsible reading of a biblical text brings to bear on it the many kinds of scholarly questions to which it will respond fruitfully and antici-

---

[9] Sandra M. Schneiders, "The Study of Christian Spirituality: Contours and Dynamics of a Discipline," *Christian Spirituality Bulletin* 6/1 (1998) 3.

pates from it the sort of depth that can contend well with the most suspicious assertions of our postmodern age, particularly those about ourselves and God. Christians share a heritage of a God made most tangible in Jesus, but such a frame does not eliminate the "Old Testament God" whom Jesus prayed to as Father. That being, highly complex across the pages of the Hebrew Bible, is mostly silent and apparently disengaged—not to say somewhat hostile—in the story of Saul.

Insofar as the relationality of God and Saul—and of course God and the community of Israel—seems characterized as seriously troubled in the text we will be reading, that is our "biblical spirituality" point of entry. How does the relationship seem to go, fail to grow, fall into disarray and neglect? Are there places where we can see other possibilities for Saul and his others, moments where our experience of ourselves and all our relationships—of whatever quality—suggest that insight, self-awareness, and change for the better can and must occur? Neither Saul nor God will be verbally fulsome about their dealings with each other, so we will need to read creatively and constructively if we are to make their opportunities work for ourselves.

A key awareness to raise as we start is what specific experience we bring to our reading. If an historian works with the story of Saul, his questions are not difficult to spot—and some will be raised here and exist in profusion among the sources cited. If a student of ancient (or modern) literature comes to the story of Saul, the specific interests sparked in her are also obvious (and available in the reading we are about to begin). Such readers have honed their sensitivities and interests by their training and lifework. But what experience do sophisticated believers bring to the text that will render them—us—quick to discern our interests there? What do we—do you—want from the story? I think we may watch for a dynamic, represented among the characters, where language offers sudden insight for characters and for readers that grows uneasily out of rueful recognition. Think of the story as filled with mirrors past which we (characters and readers) rush distractedly as we go about our daily tasks. Every now and again, though it is not our intention to scrutinize ourselves—perhaps we very much wish to avoid doing so—every now and again we catch a glimpse of ourselves from some angle and say—there I am! And the recognition, undeniable, helps us shift in some healthy way. My question for the story of Saul concerns its capacity to position for us the factors of a human dealing with a silent deity, with minimal self-knowledge, and with paltry social skills. We must literally make sense of these elements dialogically, existentially. To the extent that we engage them sensitively, existentially, answerably, the narrative will change us.

So as we begin the story of the request for a king, the repudiation of that asking, the king's demurral and then his determination, we will consider the historical circumstances of an exile community, the literary features of characters' and narrator's speech, and the existential challenge to insight, self-knowledge, and transformation. Though we have borrowed these concepts from Bakhtin, it is the careful work of biblical scholars and the methods familiar from that field of study that will assist us. How do historians reconstruct the circumstances of a community that poses a question in the sixth century? How did Hebrew storytellers or writers take advantage of the flexibility and openness of that language to draw a figure who is maddening and compelling at the same time, manipulating others as he is badly used by them too, and all under the watchful eye of God? And how do we construe the ideology or theology of these stories—their spirituality—to assist us as we stretch toward what we most desire for our lives and those of the others we love or are engaged with? Those questions will absorb us and need to be constantly rearticulated as we turn to the story of King Saul.

CHAPTER ONE

Asking a Child (1 Samuel 1–3)*

"What does having children or not have to do with the enterprise that concerns the entire book of 1 Samuel, the establishment of kingship in Israel? . . . 'The having of sons' is the image chosen by the author to convey the complicated story of how Israel comes to have kings. . . . The false start of Saul's reign is a central ideological puzzle of 1 Samuel."

Robert Polzin,
Samuel and the Deuteronomist

Occasionally I have had the potentially confusing experience of going to a movie (or renting a video) I want to see. As the sights and sounds begin, especially if they start *in medias res,* I cannot always tell whether the clip beginning is the movie I chose or one of the coming attractions being previewed for its captive audience. The matter sorts itself out eventually, but on occasion I have found myself bringing an extraneous piece of a previewed feature into the middle of the film that is finally unwinding at length before I stop myself and recall that there is no intrinsic link between the two narratives. We may experience a similar confusion as we start reading 1 Samuel. Apparently we will not meet Saul for eight biblical chapters and two of these presently written ones. But some important groundwork is being laid, and so we will include these parts of Saul's story despite the fact that he does not occur directly in them. Both so that the story can begin and so that we can pick up some genre clues, let's assume that we are treated to a few minutes of a scene—and we are not immediately sure

* This chapter contains material abridged from *How Are the Mighty Fallen,* ch. 1, to be published by Sheffield Academic Press in 2003. Reused with permission.

whether it is "our movie" or not. The characters themselves—my rescripting of them—draw our attention.[1]

Scene one: (1:1–2:11)[2] begins at a shrine in a small village called Shiloh, with five characters interacting:

Elqanah

I am off to a pretty good start, the whole thing opening with *my* family tree on the wall of our home. I, one Elqanah, man of Ramah; my lineage: Jeroham, Elihu, Tohu, Suph. In the past it has been ours to care for the ark of the covenant; so to Shiloh I still come. And, yes, my two wives, Hannah and Peninnah—Peninnah with children though Hannah with none. I am proud of my ancestors and my descendants. A man needs sons, and sons I have acquired.

Our custom, all of us, has been to go to Shiloh for worship and sacrifice to YHWH, where Eli's sons, Hophni and Phinehas, preside. When I distribute portions around, Peninnah has her share as the mother of children, but two is the best I can give Hannah, my first wife whom I love, but whom YHWH has apparently seen fit to deprive of children.[3] This situation occasions Peninnah's taunting her about YHWH's depriving Hannah of children, and then Hannah's weeping and refusing to eat. Why does she persist, to end up in tears? Frustrated myself and feeling impotent, intending to console but scarcely able to hold back my own vexation, what can I say? I finally blurt out: "'Am I not worth more to you than ten sons?'" Think of it

---

[1] My work relies on key insights of the most creative commentator on 1 Samuel, in my opinion, Robert M. Polzin, *Samuel and the Deuteronomist: A Literary Study of the Deuteronomic History: 1 Samuel* (San Francisco: Harper & Row, 1989) ch. 1.

[2] Since most of the biblical references will be to 1 Samuel, my practice throughout will be to name the book only when such is not the case; all chapter and verse references not otherwise specified are to 1 Samuel.

[3] There are two issues here: first is a textual difficulty in construing the expression for Elqanah's apportionment to Hannah. P. Kyle McCarter, *1 Samuel. A New Translation with Introduction and Commentary* (Garden City, N. Y.: Doubleday, 1980) 51–52, 60, concludes that there is no way to make sense from the Hebrew expression. It seems clear that quantity is involved, with Peninnah having more and Hannah less. The second involves the question of angle of the viewpoint on YHWH and Hannah's barrenness. By some reading conventions it is an assertion of a clearly omniscient narrator (e.g., Jan P. Fokkelman, *Narrative Art and Poetry in the Books of Samuel: Volume IV: Vow and Desire* [Assen, The Netherlands: Van Gorcum, 1993] 23–25). But once we note that this supposition about the cause of barrenness floats among several characters, with none owning the phrasing unambiguously and all concerned in the equation in some aspect, space opens up.

for once from my point of view, I advise, my words running ahead of my thinking as sometimes seems to happen when she makes me feel helpless. Cannot an actual one stand in for a theoretical ten? Cannot a husband replace a son, as a son replaces a father? Whom am I consoling, whom chiding? How many sons are enough sons? Two, or three, four? She makes no response to this query of mine, may not be brooding on it quite as I am (it probably came a little fast for her), and we go on with the feast for which we have come; she disappears for the moment. It is probably just as well; she needs to take control of herself.

When I see her again a little later that evening she is more cheerful, takes some food and drink, looks better. We all rise early next morning, finish our worship and return home, going on as before—but for whatever reason, YHWH now remembers. After some time Hannah bears a son and names him Samuel *(shĕmu'el)*, saying that she asked *(sh'l)* him of YHWH. That was part of it, no doubt. I was not so bothered as she supposed about her failure and had tried to express that, but I seem to have given way to her viewpoint. How did that happen?

I was looking forward to our next trip to Shiloh—less tension at the distribution of portions, thanks to my begetting another son—but Hannah surprises me by saying she will not be going this year. And then she *really* astonishes me: after all her desperation for this child, she announces that when he is weaned she will bring the boy to appear before YHWH and he will dwell there forever: a short time—till weaning—and a long time—forever. What is this requesting that she did, this bequesting that she has evidently done? If she thinks the child is from YHWH, then let YHWH carry on.

When we finally do go to Shiloh together to take the child, I am flabbergasted anew. It is the old priest Eli whom we find, not those sons of his; and Hannah reminds him—simultaneously and incidentally informing me—that they had recent dealings; this I did not know. She had prayed for the boy in the old man's presence. Since YHWH has granted her what she asked, she explains that she is granting him back to YHWH for all his life! Sometimes I feel as though I understand this woman little. She is confusing, contradictory. And so we leave, but not before praying additionally, words that seem to make little impression on the old priest, who just stares at her retreating back as she sings her way homeward. I feel a bit confused myself, but I catch up with her once she has finished and we go home together.

Eli

I also am introduced genealogically, first as reference for my two sons who are priests of YHWH at Shiloh, the place Elqanah the Ephraimite comes for worship and sacrifice. It seems a derivative start, my sons named to introduce me—or is it the opposite: I named to introduce them? Is this a succession story?

But my next mention is more central, for I am a priest too, sitting, positioned as a woman enters down at the end.[4] I can see her emotion, her posture of intercessory prayer, and I watch her for some time, briefly wondering what has caused her upset but mostly revolving my own thoughts in my mind, running them along a well-worn path, since I have been in place here long enough to know how things are where my sons are in charge. The eating and drinking is going on outside, and here comes a participant straggling or staggering in here. Though I can see well enough from my enthroned position high up—can certainly watch her mouth and lips—I can't really hear her voice. It must be that she is drunk—have I caught traces of her words after all: drink . . . wine . . . strong drink . . .?[5] Or is my suspicion of her condition a reading of her lips or rather rooted in what I know about the Shiloh festal liturgies? A lot of worthlessness, and it disturbs me. It can't be any waning capacities of mine, has to be her incoherent condition. I, drawing myself up on my chair, decide to speak to her about it, ask her how long she plans to go on like this—drink and wine? This sort of thing needs to be nipped in the bud, need not be tolerated. A word of censure is what is called for, and that I can do: How long will you go about drunk? Put away your wine from you. . . . Oh, well, she says it is not drinking *in* of wine at all, rather grief and vexation pouring *out*. I can only look on the outside (moving lips)—can't judge what is going on inside (grieving heart). She implies I had it exactly backwards. Not much detail about what has vexed her, but I can do what I am here to do: give her a favorable word, send her off in peace, and pray that God will give the request she has asked. That's part of my job: pronouncing and assisting God to give what people ask, encouraging them to ask what God will give. Whatever her item is I never got quite straight, nothing to do with me. She responds nicely, asks to find favor in my sight. I watch her go off, and she seems better. I can see that much, can claim that much, that she goes less distressed than she came. That is good in my view, no reason why not. I have helped her. God bless her!

---

[4] McCarter, *1 Samuel* 60–61, helpfully sketches a plausible scene for us: Hannah enters the porch of the shrine from and then returns to the room where the sacrifices are eaten; Eli is seated in the nave, where he can look either toward the porch or toward the holy of holies.

[5] I follow here the Greek translation; the Hebrew 1:11 does not have reference to wine or strong drink until Eli mentions it.

Well, days pass for me; can it be as long as she claims? For suddenly she looms up again, is here with a young bull, an ephah of flour, a skin of wine and a . . .—oh, now it is coming back: I thought she had a skinfull herself, was a skinfull herself . . .—and a young child. She is bringing him up to me, talking about that evening. She says it is the child she was interceding for. God gave her request *(sh'l)*, what she asked *(sh'l)* of him, she says. And she is granting him back *(sh'l)*, he is *sha'ul*—requested, bequested, I hear her say.[6] And I do remember that, now—all that asking in various configurations. Well, we did well. And I see the boy. Sons are a fine thing. Continuity. We count on it here at Shiloh. Did I ask for more sons? I don't remember asking, but here stands another one. Welcome, my son.

But she is not finished her jabbering yet! I do hear—too clearly this time—her words of intercession, no mumbling for these erupting cadences, high and low, barren and bearing, up and down, death and life, judges and kings. Well, I am not sure I quite get it all, but her cries leave me uncomfortable, briefly unsettled, as she disappears down the road, trailing these penetrating words behind her, the child already humming them in her absence. Nothing to do with me, so far as I can see from my stable position here. Women's genre, this triumphal poetry. Well, there goes the man as well, and I see the boy stays, a little minister to Yhwh before me, the priest.

Peninnah

Poor Hannah, no children. Bad enough for her at Ramah, worse at Shiloh, my portions according to fruitfulness drawing attention to her dearth. She finds more reproach in me than I intend, hears more than I say.[7] But on

---

[6] The wordplay for these names is complex and ubiquitous and can be laid out, though scarcely resolved. The asking/Saul puns occur in 1:12, 17, 20, 27, 28 (three times). For more detail on the etymologies and wordplays consult Fokkelman, *Desire* 56–59, McCarter, *1 Samuel* 62–64, Polzin, *Samuel and the Deuteronomist* 24–25. Everett Fox, *Give Us A King! Samuel, Saul and David* (New York: Schocken, 1999) 9, translates "Saul" as "lent on request."

[7] Peninnah, of course, says nothing in the biblical story; the narrator summarizes a pattern of behavior, using two verbs (for vex and thunder) and the highly ambiguous syntax that can be read to signify both purpose and result—a big difference in English. To add to the ambiguity there are neither proper names nor freestanding pronouns to indicate who is subject and who object of the transaction. Hannah refers to her vexation in 1:16. It is a highly diagnostic place in the text for all readers. It is possible to view the scene as two squabbling rivals setting off a long-suffering husband, but that is not the only possibility. Even if we may think it a likely assumption from a patriarchal culture, I at least want to counter it here rather than reinscribe it unconsciously in my own reading.

this one particular occasion I do sort of let loose some remarks, not so much to taunt as to goad her into something other than self-pity. Why she is childless is not mine to figure; if it has to do with Elqanah, she needs to take care of it with him, not blame me. If it is YHWH who has withheld her from bearing, well, I wouldn't know what to say about that, hers to sort out as best she can.[8] But she needs to *do something!* I wonder if *she* knows fully why she is weeping, what she builds up to year after year as we go through this ritual. She waits for this moment to come and then wades into it too fatalistically, too determinedly. Our husband has no idea that his conspicuous counting-out only makes it worse. Maybe my tossing some vexatious snapping will help her move; at least it removes her gloominess and tears and refusal of food from what is supposed to be a celebration. That's not so bad an achievement for a few words. I wonder where she's gone?

Hannah

I enter silent this story of sons, of succession, begin as a failure; a man with a lineage and two wives, one of whom is childrened—makes my lack of bearing, my empty womb, most prominent. For all I seem able to manage, Elqanah's line will come to an end at me—and who knows what will become of *me,* with no son to care for me.

My condition weighs on my mind and of course it upsets me. It can only be, or seem, my fault—unless it is YHWH who has closed my womb as some assert, but who is to know the difference?[9] YHWH says no to me, has not said yes to me about sons. Why? I am a beloved wife but not a mother of sons. Peninnah becomes as though first wife with her children, while I, though first, become like a secondary one. I stand between Peninnah, my adversary—who makes pilgrimage feasting an opportunity to vex me over my sonlessness, and Elqanah—who gives me a double portion nonetheless as well as some words about my condition—or lack of it. The apportionment, if not the sonlessness and the vexing, gets to me on these occasions. I build up my dread the moment of his—granted, unintended—emphasis of my

---

[8] Again, Hannah does not blame Peninnah explicitly. My point here is to raise the question of whose assessment it is that YHWH is responsible for Hannah's barrenness by showing that none of the characters actually claims it. It is usually construed as a narrator-omniscient remark, hence reliably true, but I am handling it differently, with a Bakhtinian and feminist methodology.

[9] Character discourse calls attention to the social undertow when values are ascribed to YHWH; when God is an invisible but interpreted actor on the human stage and in the human realm, when things do not go according to the putative divine will, blame will tend to be apportioned.

deficiency, lose my joy in worship of the God who has, they say, closed my womb; I find, as usual, my desire for the feast's eating and drinking vanished.

Elqanah's self-centering words finally penetrate my isolation: his voice asking me why I weep, why I do not eat, why I am sad; he lists well the externals: my weeping, fasting, mourning! Does he really want to know why I act as I do? His solution, a substitution pushed too readily, is himself. He is, in his scanning view, starting from his position as a father, worth more than ten sons. But that cannot be so from where my eyes start. One half-husband cannot possibly be better than ten sons. I must ask for sons, for something. I turn silently from Elqanah in search of one who can be more helpful.

Rising while the others are eating and drinking, I approach the darkened shrine, glimpsing at the edge of my vision the old priest Eli, seated on his thronechair; but I have not much interest in his elderly presence. It is not he who has prevented me from bearing sons, nor him with whom I must intercede about what I am lacking. *His* two sons are no help to my lack. Distressed, barren, hungry, whispering, weeping, I vow my vow, my tears and distress wrapping around my repeating intercession: YHWH Sebaoth, see, please—take sight of the distress of your maidservant, remember me and do not forget your maidservant and give your maidservant seed of men; then I will give him to YHWH all the days of his life. . . .[10] I was beseeching in just that vein, beginning to hear more clearly the source of my sorrow, when a voice came wafting out from the priest's chair—asking how long I would go drunken . . . urging that I should put away my wine. . . . The accusation caught me quite by surprise, since I had eaten and drunk nothing, but was praying and whispering and vowing to YHWH, surely not even audibly enough for the old man seated at a distance to hear. And he clearly did not *hear*—whatever he *saw* made him think me drunken. I answered politely, mentioning that I was a woman straitened of spirit, not drinking in wine but pouring out my whole self before YHWH. I asked, hoping to seem courteous but needing also to counter his obvious inference, that he not consider me a disorderly daughter, for out of an abundance of anxiety and vexation had I been speaking. Well, he surely did not ask to hear any detail about my distress or vexation, but quickly assured me that I could go in peace, sent me off with the usual formulaic word that the God of Israel might grant my asking *(sh'l)* which I had asked *(sh'l)*. Not knowing what

---

[10] One of my "test readers" questioned why Hannah should be so willing to give back a son, should assume that God would be desirous of it. There are several possible ways to approach that excellent question, but one is that the unreality simply underlines the fact that we are not witnessing a realistic scene but an artifice.

else to say, and feeling there was no point in staying longer, I asked, also formulaic but sincere, to find favor in his eyes—and left; oddly, I did feel better and ate and drank some festal portion with Elqanah that night.

It was an odd experience of intercession, strangely interrupted, but the old priest's words—first correcting but then reassuring me from his secure and distanced perch—cheered me more than Elqanah's similar ones, whether he knew what he was saying or not. Or was it my own words that I have taken comfort in? I think perhaps that comes closer to it. They all think it is sonlessness that makes me mope, and I thought so too, think so still. But when I was in that place of intercession I asked God to see me, to look on my distress, to remember, not to forget. Bruised from being passed among a Job's trio who think they understand my tears but have mostly seen themselves and their own reflected surfaces, I hear myself *asking to be seen.*[11] In the asking I get something at once, some insight into what I have been lacking even more than a baby. The participation in something reciprocal is what I want, feel I have been given already. We finished our worship early next morning and went home again, and Elqanah knew me and YHWH remembered and I conceived and bore a son and I called his name Samuel *(shmu'el),* since from YHWH I asked *(sh'l)* him. What I asked I immediately recycled, but it is with me still.

It was too soon time to journey to Shiloh again, so I simply told Elqanah that I would not be going this year: when the child is weaned I will bring him up so that he may appear before the face of YHWH and dwell there forever. I admitted only then to Elqanah what I had vowed to YHWH under the feeble watch of Eli: given to God at Shiloh forever, to appear there. Elqanah seemed surprised but said I should do what seemed best to me—stay home until he is weaned? take him up later? leave him in service forever? (a bit incoherent); only may YHWH raise up his word. I am not quite sure I understood what he meant by that, not having heard any particular words of YHWH to rise or fall. Elqanah and Eli talk alike, poor dears, sort of pious boilerplate that hangs in the air, pointless, generic, and vapid. In both cases one wonders if they know what they are pronouncing about. But in any case my intervention was effective, and I remained apart from Shiloh, its priests and sacred spaces until the boy was weaned; and then we brought him up and offered the sacrifice as required. I reminded the old priest who I was, tried to inflate a bit the role he played in the getting of the child, but he gazed wordlessly at me, perhaps not hearing or

---

[11] Polzin's manner of watching shared language reminds us about the looking at appearances/discerning the heart distinction that emerges later in the story (*Samuel and the Deuteronomist* 27, 49).

perceiving what I was saying to him. It did not matter. I said in his presence what I needed to say: "'I interceded with YHWH and he gave, the boy I requested *(sh'l)* of YHWH I am now bequesting to *(sh'l)* YHWH—he is bequested/*sha'ul*.'" I think my formula, so carefully rehearsed, was intended to go over his head in any case. And so it did.

But I suddenly had more to say; words rushed through me, and I sang them out loud and clear enough for the deaf to hear as I left the boy. Whose words these also are I do not know. Given me from the past, they became mine briefly, and I cast them forth for others to claim as well. My song's main motion is reversal. My heart that was grieving now leaps up, raised by YHWH the rock who gives me speech against opponents who talk and think for me; my words address those high up: no need to multiply arrogance and windy ignorance from lofty perches: those who sit up high, take note! God reverses, subverts, averts: warriors' bow breaks weak, feeble gird on strength; the stuffed hire themselves out to eat, but the hungry fatten, batten; the barren has seven, the mother becomes forlorn. Extinguishing, enlivening is YHWH's to do, lowering to *sheol* and lifting out, disinheriting some and enriching others, leveling some down, levering others up, raising the poor from the dust, lifting the needy from the refuse heap so *they* can sit on thrones, honored with princes. Is a surprise in store for those who have sat on such thrones for ages, gathering in more than they have given out? How can I claim these powerful shifts as YHWH's, or God manage them? YHWH owns the pillars on which earth's edges are set (more high places prone to wracking!).

Where does such a song well up from, where does it head? It is my experience and my hope come to the boil, pushed until I thundered forth like God. Some phrases are familiar—so I borrowed them from the common stock, I suppose; but the song was freshly born of what I have been through: the barrenness, the denigration, the rivalry, the asking, the rescue, the bearing, the weaning, the bringing, the explaining, the sacrificing and the leaving Samuel are where the song came from. No one made any response to it! Elqanah, rooted while I went out singing, finally ran after me, catching up with me about the time the song quit; but the boy remains at Shiloh, with YHWH and with Eli, seated on his special chair. I know he heard me clearly this time and sense why he risks no benedictory colophon to *these* words of mine.

YHWH

Cultic ritual goes on at Shiloh, where Hophni and Phinehas, of Eli's line, are priests, purportedly to me, though I doubt the thought often crosses their minds. Elqanah sacrifices there as well and distributes portions around to his family, makes it two for the childless Hannah, whose womb has yet to bear the son she so desires; for I have closed her womb, or so "they" say. So do they all come up to my place regularly, and there do they reenact this family drama of fertility and infertility, of satiety and dearth, as they perform the sacrifice under the eyes of the inattentive or too-attentive priests. One year gives way to the next. I, too, am attentive if not apparently too responsive; responsive to what? I have not been asked yet. No one has thought to *ask* me, to ask *me*.

But one evening when Eli is seated and dozing in the place that has long been his and where his fathers have sat before him (and his sons envision sitting after he is gone) a needy woman enters the shrine as well; behind her the sacrifice has been performed and portions are being consumed; all are content except the one who is weeping, fasting, sad in heart. Why is she approaching me, her hands extending empty between herself and the ark that makes tangible my presence? She speaks with me, vowing me a vow and asking me to look, to see, to remember and not to forget (requests I am easy to hit up for) and to give her conception; she in turn promises her child to me all his days. A prayer offered out of regular sequence, sent forth from empty hands, spoken by the woman with no assistance asked from the priest, said directly and in her own phrasing. They all think this is about sons, sons they all want desperately and from me. But there is more; the tears of this woman are also about lacking, about asking, asking and receiving, receiving and giving back, giving back and asking again. So it is about the economy of relationship underlying the bartered particularities.[12] A lack, intensified by what she thinks is a triple miscuing of those who read it, begins to be unraveled by the one who feels it. Her words make more visible, strip down and show more clearly what she lacks besides a child as she brings that neediness before me. Hannah's inadequacy is not simply an empty womb; the need she feels has been already remedied is something deeper than that, a richness enclosing herself that will soon contain what she has asked. If there were not more remedied than a son, why does she feel better as she leaves? She is not pregnant yet, nor does she likely place too much confidence in Eli's word. I have not reacted in any clear way. But she has started something with me that gratifies her. Brought in by one need, she goes out with a transaction that will take some work. I think that is what she wants: a relationship; me too.

---

[12] Like Peninnah, YHWH has no direct discourse in this section of narrative but, unlike her, God obviously has much more scope in the Hebrew Bible. That God wants more than routine or external observance is a support beam of the divine character, and I draw on it here.

Once they are home I do "remember" and she does conceive. I had not really forgotten. It is a matter of careful timing, this joint venture we share responsibility for. But I will always choose my times with care. I am patient, up to a point: attentive and eventually responsive. But I like to collaborate. I like being asked by those who acknowledge a need, who see their own efforts in need of supplement.

When eventually she brings him up to Shiloh, this time with an offering as prescribed, she then tells Eli what had passed between us and how *I* had done what *she* asked, and how *she* is now doing to *me* what she vowed she would do. We share the requesting and donating of the child, Hannah and I. The child is and will remain our common project, however it may appear to any attending, and whether it turns out to have been a good plan or not. Elqanah and Eli simply stare at her, the child as well. I, as asked, see her and the child, who now appears before me. And then borrowing words from me she sings for him, for any with ears.[13] Whose words? She pours me into her language, my powerful works into her provocative poetry, my old word-deeds into her fresh experience. Hannah is able to get me to do what she wants, and she is reciprocally responsive to me. Her empty self—closed womb, as some would put it—reaches to me again from the cultic site. She opens her mouth, mine as well, speaking of me and of my projects what is true, discerning in her own experiences a rhythm that is intentional, designed.

Comment

What has the been the purpose of presenting such a preview, what the gain from it? First, the presentation of the ruminations of these characters has brought out both multiple interconnections within their discourse and simultaneously the various disjunctions. They are all talking about the same thing—the request for a son—but they seem more separated than united in their asking, at least as I have set it up. Second, the Hebrew verb for asking *(sh'l),* played with repeatedly, sets up a extended wordplay on the "asked" son who will be king: Saul—in Hebrew *sha'ul:* King Saul's asking.[14] Third, the social valence of discourse variety has been made

---

[13] Hannah's words that close this scene are commonly credited as being an inspired prophecy. She speaks as one privy to the court of God and as one who sees ahead into the centuries of monarchy that lie ahead of Israel.

[14] This point is potentially confusing and so needs additional emphasis. What has been asked is a son, all the wordplay around him signaling that he is "requested," hence linked to Saul. But this is not the birth story of the actual Saul, but of the child Samuel, hence his name and persona in the story are Samuel, not Saul. The storyteller is struggling to connect but not conflate them.

visible by my reading. You might do it differently; the openness of the language permits a variety of possibilities, not infinite but wide. And yet I would defend the validity of my reading of their language, would answer for it. Fourth, the hypothesis of the genre as a riddle or parable has been developed. The scene is not simply a transparent and truth-bearing window onto a family gathering; rather, it is a carefully constructed vignette which shapes the dynamics we will witness throughout 1 Samuel. One character desires what she lacks, what others around her have. Her desire is countered variously but ultimately abetted, granted with varying awareness on the part of those going along with it: husband, priest, co-wife, deity. How pleased all will be ultimately remains to be seen, but the woman's words of celebration (moving into the genres of prophetic speech and poetry) suggest a direction.

The dynastic amplitude surrounding Elqanah insensitizes him to the need for Hannah's quest. He is co-opted into it, cluelessly though not incidentally. What he is—son and father—makes him shortsighted. His words show that he quickly loses control over the small part in the asking process he had. Eli, similarly attended by forebears and heirs, also miscues, as his speech makes plain. But his failing will not develop simply as myopia but into a more willful blindness. His language shows him project onto others what he does not face in himself and censures the innocent woman rather than his sons, more needy of it. Though he pronounces on the request, and thus becomes part of it, he is never shown to have understood it. Peninnah, a third character with sons, provokes, but her motive is shown potentially multiple and hence undecidable. I aim with her to counter the stereotype of women fighting over men and babies, but the role in which Peninnah is cast here underlines the factions prominent in the requesting process. What these three share, besides sons, is their own sense of need for more, granted that they accede to that concern on Hannah's part.

Hannah's words show her as wanting something, the precise nature of which is not so easily pinpointed. That misunderstandings accompany her whole transaction is key, granted that her familiars acquiesce, each distinctively, to what she asks. That is, without fully "getting" what Hannah desires, other characters assist her, add their efforts to hers. That she wants a child does not say all of what she asks, nor must the oddity of turning him over before he even arrives elude us. She seems too quick, perhaps, to promise that the request will not disarrange the status quo. Her request sails out clearly, helped by a mediator she may not have required. The prompt for it is multi-stranded: she lacks what another has, in fact what everyone else has. Some sons seem neutral, though Eli's will also prove lethal. Her son comes late and will go early. The silence of YHWH makes the divine zone much more opaque. That God is spoken *about,* referred *to,* invoked formulaically by the "dynasts" (Elqanah and Eli) need not add up to reliable speech about him. How Hannah talks to and of God—comes needy and borrows old words of God—is somewhat at cross-purposes to what others say. God is imaged by the various approaches made, and these do not add together so coherently. What seems clearest is that Hannah's words get through and are reciprocated not only by the request granted but by the gift of prophecy as well. The greatest uncertainty or ambiguity for us to note comes over allegations about God's role in the presence and absence of the child. What God does can be rumored and alleged but loses its crisp certainty when the characters discuss it. The narrator's collusion with the characters diminishes any confidence in omniscience. Though we will not again have occasion to fill out the characters' consciousnesses in just this way—in fact, I will take pains not to do so—here it has served the central purpose of exposing the spaciousness of discourse, its capacity to hold various interpretations.

Scene two (2:12–3:21) continues at the Shiloh shrine:

Though there are indications that the parabolic genre (as Polzin calls this type of *mashal*), continues, we can negotiate its fundamental dynamics in a more straightforward way. I suggest that there are two moves most emphasized in this section: the repudiation of one dynastic line and the formation of a new son. After setting forth these two vectors we will return to see how this second scene emphasizes certain elements from the first scene.

First, the dynasty of Eli—not only the two wicked priests Hophni and Phinehas but also their father and in fact the whole line—is scathingly rebuked. The narrator describes the priestly ministry of the two sons in a way that emphasizes its radical evil. If we understand cult—Shiloh's as well as public worship in general—to be a medium of relatedness between God and human beings in which priests have a catalyzing role we can appreciate the enormity of the sins of the two young Elides. Rather than care properly for the goods brought by worshipers, the two priests intervene in the sacrifice to spear meat for themselves at a tender moment and brush off the complaints of any who counter or plead with them; thus the priests serve themselves instead of, and even from, the goods that were to flow between worshipers and worshiped. They abuse female cult personnel in a way we scarcely need belabor, the implication being that their sacerdotal authority is made to serve the sexual violations (2:12-17, 22-25).[15] The old Eli is first

---

[15] David Jobling, *1 Samuel* (Collegeville: The Liturgical Press, 1998) 134, urges that we see these abuses as endemic, not simply occasional. If he is right it reinforces the sense that a big picture is being drawn for us of a crisis in worship, not simply a local disorder.

unable and finally unwilling to rebuke his sons, the blindness he demonstrated when dealing with Hannah seeming to extend to matters nearer
home (2:22-5; 3:18).

His wrong seems perhaps less than that of his sons, but the man of God
who looms up at the Shiloh shrine to deliver God's word does not release
the father from blame (2:27-36). This disembodied prophetic voice makes
several points: First, though the Elide family had long served as priests—
from Egypt, the man reminds them—they are fired; and though they had
been promised service forever, that word is revoked, destroyed as it has
been by the violations of the priests. Moreover, those violations are pronounced in cultic language: Eli is charged with having honored/fattened[16]
his greedy-eyed sons by condoning their grabbing even more than was
already reserved for them. The honor they had previously enjoyed will turn
to contempt, their plenty to penury, and those who wielded sacrificial forks
will die by the sword. There are numerous difficulties of one sort or another in the prophetic speech, but the tenor of it is clear enough. In a final
point, though the line will diminish it will not be quite cut off: a remainder
from the Elide family will beg for a crust of bread from the new line to be
set in place of the Elides. Sign of all this? The death of Hophni and Phinehas
on the same day. Far from an arbitrary punishment, the deaths attest openly
to the rottenness of the line.

There is no response to this oracle on the part of Eli or his sons, no shift
in their behavior. And so God intervenes again. In a night vision (or audi-
tion) to the young Samuel, God repeats more succinctly the condemnation
of the Elides (3:11-14). The old priest's refusal to stop what he knows to be
happening at the shrine is beyond expiation or toleration. Eli's passivity in
response to these words again ends a scene (3:18). The narrator has told us
prior to both of these dramatic interventions that the refusal of the priestly
house to reverse the corruption of their heritage is now bound with God's
determination to eliminate them (2:25).[17] It is a harsh statement, even as we
remember that we are working in an imprecise genre where something

---

[16] The Hebrew verbal root *kbd* conveys both the notion of honor and the sense of physical heaviness. Though it may seem an odd blend to us, we might reach back to an earlier era
(or to another culture) when a portly gentleman seems distinguished by his *avoirdupois* or a
Victorian woman's physical attainments, well-corseted and buttressed, are part of her august
presence. To be spindly suggests undernourishment.

[17] The prophet Ezekiel, writing in the sixth century, which I am proposing as key for the
production or urgent address of our story, dialogues with this narrator viewpoint that God
desires the death of Hophni and Phinehas by quoting God as saying: "For I have no pleasure
in the death of anyone, says the LORD God. Turn [convert, repent], then and live" (Ezek
18:32).

does and does not resemble something with which it is juxtaposed. We are working with a riddle: are dynastic sons a viable solution to Israel's leadership crisis in the sixth century? Can ancient promises be seen as entitlements when those receiving them have been proven not only unfaithful but destructive over time? Are foundational violations of the leadership easily reversed? The answer to all of these queries seems to be "no."

The second major point made clear in this short section arises from the contrast between the newly requested and bequested Samuel and the Elide scions (2:12-26): the abusive priests and the young child clothed by his mother's gift of a robe, which enhances the priestly garment he wears; Eli's sons at odds with God and people while the young Samuel is approved by deity and community. And yet we must also ask whether Samuel's formation at Shiloh amid Elides can be sufficiently, or even minimally, healthful. There is no answer to this question, at least not presently. To put the matter in structural rather than in personal terms: can the new son be a replacement for the discredited ones? The oracle of the man of God raises the same question, especially as it speaks of the faithful priest who will be raised up and from whom the Elides will beg their coins and crusts (2:35-36). Is Samuel the faithful priest? It seems so from the perspective of this chapter, and yet the story will have more to say on the point.

As we move to conclude, we can converge the points made in the voicings of the characters in what I called section one (1:1–2:11) with the events of our section two (2:12–3:21). We have been shown, I think, that both lacking sons and having them causes a crisis. Sons are a solution, but they are also the problem. Sons are taken: Hannah's son is given over by her, and he is only the first of a series of sons taken and sons taking. The man of God has already indicated that the two sons of Eli are about to fall on the same day, and they will take others down with them. Eli is indicted for the deeds of his sons, and their collapse is not unrelated to his condoning of their sins. The question of God's complicity in the sons and the sonlessness must also be reviewed in this story that will turn out to be as much about God as it is about Saul. The narrator, whether in his own voice or as reporting the viewpoints of characters, alleges that the withholding of sons is God's doing. No one in the story contradicts that truism about God; it remains a staple of biblical studies. But a more careful look cautions us: Elqanah's distribution of sacrificial portions is attended by the voiced suggestion that God is responsible for Hannah's barrenness, and Peninnah's vexing fertility is the second occasion that provokes the remark that God had prevented Hannah's conception. But Elqanah is thoroughly discredited as an exegete of Hannah's own perceptions, and Peninnah vanishes before we can get at her viewpoint more thoroughly. That Eli credits God with providing offspring (1:17; 2:20-21) is both a boilerplate response and in any case wafted toward Hannah with other misinformation. Does God withhold sons? Does God will to send them? It is less clear than it seems at the surface. In this riddle, where to ask sons will be to request kings, we need to observe with great care. The removal of the sons will be similarly suggestive, I think. Is God determined to eliminate the Elides? The point is urged but nested among many other reasons for the line's collapse. Filial incorrigibility, paternal complacence invalidate their role. And yet the Elides will not vanish so summarily as it sounds here. God's role regarding dynastic sons is ambiguous, even permissive.

Related is the question of Hannah's tears (1:3-18): why does she weep? Her tears pool around her lack of offspring and seem remedied when she bears. She exults in the reversal of her distress, credited clearly to God (2:1-10). But again, have we been faked out? Hannah's husband Elqanah reads her tears as a reproach of himself, and his solipsistic solution to her infertility is himself. Feminist criticism has deconstructed his viewpoint and made its angle clear. The priest Eli mistakes Hannah's tears as part of the disorder that more nearly describes the priest's sons. So Eli reads Hannah's tears as poorly as Elqanah does. Hannah does not discourse on them directly, but when she does speak she gives us our first access to a crucial insight we will see repeatedly throughout the story of Saul. The relationality between deity and people is more focal than any particular mode or circumstance of it. That is, the vitality of the relationship between God and humans is more central than any way in which it is expressed. If we stop to think about it we might come to the same conclusion in friendships that we value deeply. Circumstances will, must change, and they will always structure a relationship. But if some way of staying close, let's say summer vacations spent together, deteriorates into a mere form or a burden and begins to erode rather than refresh a friendship, then it is in trouble. So here Hannah asks to be seen by God, who responds. The son is a way of Hannah's asking God for what she lacks. The son she asks she is willing to give back. The requesting and bequesting of the child resembles the cultic economy that the Elides are thwarting: people bring their produce with which God has blessed them, offer it and receive it back so that they may rejoice in the relationship. Sons, priests—and eventually a king—are appointed to serve this basic relationship of God and Israel, the "one thing needful," which is what I will call this insight so we can tag it when it recurs.

So the son has been asked, granted, but his presence is shadowed. Have we seen an extraneous snippet from some coming attraction or is this set of vignettes really a part of the story of Saul? It may not be convincing to you yet that asking sons is asking kings, but can you hold a place for the thesis among your other questions? The etiology of the asking does not fully coincide with the particular baby produced; his name, after all, is not *"Shaʾul"* but Samuel. Whether sons are a solution or a problem is left in the balance. One of the most characteristic features of the Hebrew text as we have it is a sense of repetition: something is stated and then resaid in slightly different but closely similar terms. The Hebrew word for images, riddles, proverbs *(mashal)* works in just this way. One thing is like another, is laid beside it so we can see the similarities and differences. What is your sense that the story we have entered functions like a riddle? Does the speech of the characters, closely observed now, enhance your sense that we are seeing something less natural than a scene, not realistic but more artifice-like? Has our play with the discourse of these characters showed you some ways to read their speech more critically, bringing to your attention more options for understanding it? And finally, and most important—though wholly intertwined with the other questions just posed—do you have a sense of engagement with the story yet? Can you read it not simply as a museum piece giving access to a past era, not even reverentially as a biblical story, but as something that engages you? I would be disappointed were you to conclude, crudely and allegorically, that we are "like" Hannah, like Eli, or resemble the lawless sons. But has the narration sparked anything in you, and if so, how did it happen? What is your sense of God so far in the story, and how do you account for it? Questions are what make this story go, so remember to shepherd those you sense unfolding as the story proceeds.

CHAPTER TWO

Seeking a Refuge (1 Samuel 4–7)

"The ark is uniquely endowed to raise the primary question pervading the entire ark story: who is to be Israel's/the Lord's proper caretaker? . . . How to get the people Israel and the lost ark back to the land of Israel after the disaster of the exile is central to the story's subject matter."

Robert Polzin,
Samuel and the Deuteronomist

In the first chapter of this work we worked from the presumption that the scenes from the opening of the book of 1 Samuel, especially those clustering around the much-sought child, function like a riddle. To make that assumption explicit—whether in the end you agree with it or not—is important, since it frees us from assuming without reflection that we have a realistic narrative that is telling us something historical or quasi-factual. Again, it is like hearing a joke. If someone grabs us by the lapels and says "An elephant went into the cigar store . . ." we might rush to assist (or to escape). When alerted to jocular tone and circumstances we anticipate a joke and need not wonder how the animal wedged itself in the door, whether it was carrying money for a purchase, and so forth. The words are not different, but we slot them into a different genre, and that makes all the difference. Insofar as we operate on the assumption or hypothesis that the asking of sons is like the asking for a king and have registered the insistence of that request from a number of voices, we have keyed to what I consider to be the book of 1 Samuel's primary task: to propose a riddle for consideration in the sixth century: shall we try to reestablish royal rule after the exile in Babylon or not? Getting both the question and the answer—which is a resounding "no!"—is central to the story of Saul. Saul is the riddle, the question—as his name suggests in Hebrew—and the answer.

In this chapter we are dealing with another parabolic "preview" of the attraction coming in our next chapter: the asking and granting of a king. Though some scholars disagree and classify the ark story as a remnant of some other unit oddly incorporated here, if we attend to genre considerations it won't seem quite so anomalous or require explanation as intrusive in our story. This *is* our narrative, and our challenge is to make sense of it. To do so we will listen again to how the discourse runs here as characters interact, so that the conversations are a bit denaturalized. And finally we will look at the question of answerability for the relationship between God and people and suggest the vital minimum required. For ease of reference we can work with this material in three sections: the ark's main adventures and discourse comprising those scenes (4:1-7:1), reserving for the end a small piece relating news of its capture back at the Shiloh shrine (4:12-22), and the aftermath as Samuel and the people try to get on track again (7:2-17).

The riddle of the ark's adventures (4:1–7:1)

Three preliminary points are apt here: First, there seems to be a gap between the end of the story of Samuel's maturing into leadership and this next event of battle with an enemy. He is absent throughout the story of the ark. Leadership is in the hands of Eli's renegade sons Hophni and Phinehas. Dearth of leaders *is* the problem. Samuel's absence and Elides' presence each highlight the leadership problem from distinct angles. It helps continue to focus us on the question of "the asked son": is Samuel, "the *sha'ul*," the appropriate leader or not? So whether he is absent or present, we are questioning whether he can lead well or not—and why.

A second point for early consideration is the nature of the ark of God, which is the central character in this episode. It is not so difficult to line up biblical information about what the ark "was,"[1] but we have to think about the elephant in the cigar store again. For the ark is more than its most obvious self, a container for the law tablets as specified in Deuteronomy 10 and 31. It is not less than that container, but it has some additional identity as

---

[1] For a summary of the ark throughout the Bible consult C. L. Seow, "Ark of the Covenant," *Anchor Bible Dictionary,* ed. David Noel Freedman (New York: Doubleday, 1992) 1:386–93. My characterization here rises from the ark's presence in the books that seem to be part of the Deuteronomistic History, which includes 1 Samuel.

well as it moves in time and space. In Joshua 3–4 the ark first led and then followed the community across the Jordan River into the land and was carried ceremoniously in the defeat of Jericho (ch. 6); it vanishes from there, to surface at Bethel (Judg 20:27). We find it next at Shiloh, witness to the deeds of the Elides and to the condemnation of those deeds by the man of God and then by YHWH directly and to a promise awaiting time and space to ripen. As will be argued in more detail below, how to conceive the ark's identity is a major part of the problem, not simply for characters but for commentators and readers as well. I think it is best named as representing specifically the relationality of YHWH and Israel, that is, the web of mutual commitments they have undertaken, the bonds holding them both together and in tension. The ark is not simply a surrogate for the deity, a sort of stand-in *tremendum,* nor simply a people's valued palladium. Like the cult at Shiloh, the ark is a tangible meeting place of God and people, a site where their mutual and intersecting fidelity (or the lack of it) will be put to the test. Though about to go temporarily offscreen, it will occasionally appear in the longer story winding past Saul, becoming first part of David's cultic establishment, then disappearing into Solomon's temple from which it evidently goes off to destruction or exile with the people in the sixth century. The ark is constructed in terms of how that symbol—the material marker of the YHWH/Israel relationship—is handled: abusively, ignorantly, reverently, cultically, and so forth.

Another "new" character needs a quick introduction here: the Philistines. Again, without bogging down on the historical Philistines,[2] we can see that in this story they are presented and function as a foreign "other," dreaded and despised. They are a small but mighty near neighbor, threatening in a variety of ways intermittently since the days of the judges, which is the period we are still in prior to the choice of a king. The Philistines menace Israel from the southwest edge of the area known today as Gaza.

---

[2] War with the Philistines runs from Judges 13 or so (or even sooner) until David defeats them conclusively (when they cease to be mentioned so regularly); hence they are the main foe represented as the judges period gives way to kings. They are the intermittent external foe for that time—taking land from Israel but never losing their own cities (at least not the key five). For a recent historical reconstruction of this rather maligned group see Trude Dothan and Moshe Dothan, *People of the Sea: The Search for the Philistines* (New York: Macmillan, 1992) who review in a very readable format the story of the investigation of the Philistines in terms of broad Ancient Near Eastern culture. They are thus a plausible opponent in the period in which they are set in 1 Samuel as well as memorable in the period in and for which the text is produced. For a discussion of how they have been carried from the pejorative treatment they have in the Bible into our broader cultural context see David Jobling, *1 Samuel* (Collegeville: The Liturgical Press, 1998) Part IV.

With those points in mind, we can see at once the significance of what happens. When the Philistines and Israelites muster and face off between Aphek and Ebenezer, the first battle results in defeat for Israel. The elders, reaching for both an explanation and a remedy, order the ark from Shiloh. For the ark to be objectified as a magical palladium is wholly inappropriate with the identity I have suggested for it above; a relationship is not a magical talisman. When the ark arrives it is managed by Hophni and Phinehas, about whom we have heard nothing good and plenty bad. They are poor shepherds of the relationship between God and people, and their malevolent incompetence is about to send God-and-people into exile. The beleaguered Israelites are glad to see the ark while the Philistines are correspondingly dismayed; the Philistines are galvanized by their fear of the ark's deity and the Israelites are arguably smug. The smug are defeated by the galvanized. The second slaughter of Israelites is greater than the first: thirty thousand die, including the two Elide priests. Worst of all, the ark is captured by the Philistines.

Skipping for the moment the bringing of the news to Shiloh, we follow the ark into exile. It has very odd adventures, described at length in 1 Samuel 5–6. Mikhail Bakhtin has a good word for us here, a useful concept: the chronotope.[3] A chronotope is the blending—or an acknowledgment of the inseparability—of time and space. Not simply the same as setting (though including it), the chronotope also calls attention to the angle or viewpoint from which consciousness is portrayed. The most relevant chronotope here is exile, a concept that involves space away from home and time in the future, as marked from the experience of the ark. Parabolically we are given a fast-forward into the early sixth century, where the relationality of God and Israel is wrenched from its accustomed place to dwell among foreigners. The Philistines are the group whose angle is verbally given, but the ark is shown reactive to misuse. While in Ashdod the ark is placed in a temple before the Philistine god Dagon; its presence

[3] In his essay "Forms of Time and of the Chronotope in the Novel," *The Dialogic Imagination: Four Essays,* edited by Michael Holquist, translated by Caryl Emerson and Michael Holquist (Austin: University of Texas Press, 1981), Bakhtin wrote: "We will give the name *chronotope* (literally 'time space') to the intrinsic connectedness of temporal and spatial relationships that are artistically expressed in literature" (p. 84, emphasis in original). His other famous saying, added later to that same essay, is more metaphorical but perhaps more suggestive: "What is the significance of all these chronotopes? What is most obvious is their meaning for *narrative*. They are the organizing centers for the fundamental narrative events of the novel. The chronotope is the place where the knots of narrative are tied and untied. It can be said without qualification that to them belongs the meaning that shapes narrative" (p. 250, emphasis in original).

topples Dagon—whether in a posture of reverence or defeat—and when the Philistines do not get the implications of their god's first tumble, he falls again and sustains additional damage (and calls attention to the chronotope of falling, already articulated for us by Hannah's song of praise, where the mighty fall). As the ark is sent out of one catastrophic situation into another, mice, tumors, and panic multiply, until finally everyone concedes that the ark is a dangerous guest.

The challenge now for the ark's captors is how to return it. Again reserving comment on their conversations for later, we can notice here an extreme care to let the ark have its own way, to be guided from some desire beyond the human. The Philistines devise a process that maximizes the disincentive for it to go back to Israel: that is, by delegating its transportation to two nursing cows unaccustomed to the yoke they are asked to bear, by their nonetheless pulling together in a direction away from their offspring, the Philistines show it unlikely that the ark returns to Israel by chance. That the captors of "God and Israel" also send the ark back with gifts—totally odd at the level of realism, this inclusion of golden mice and swellings—it makes sense at the level of riddle, calling our attention to the other instances of release from captivity.[4] The story is shown for a time from the eyes of the Philistines who have followed at a distance to watch developments. What we see them see is the arrival of the ark at Beth Shemesh, its joyful reception by the inhabitants of that place, who offer a sacrifice of thanksgiving (thus obviating the need to return cart and cows). If the ark were a Winnebago it would by now have a lot of decals from its travels and more to collect before retiring eventually to Jerusalem. The ark, chronotopically speaking, is mobile (until it disappears for the last time into the Temple). But we can see that the ark's return to its own land (conspicuously not to Shiloh) trips off a fresh leadership crisis.

That problem develops, outside the purview of the foreigners but related for us, when the homecoming does not continue unproblematically. Slaughter occurs among Beth Shemeshites so that these "indigenous," like those of Ashdod, Gath, and Ekron, are no longer eager to have the ark. That is, the ark again reacts to a welcome that is somehow wrong, though in just what aspect we cannot say. In any case, the ark is taken up to Kiriath-jearim, a city near Jerusalem, where a man with a priestly name (Abinadab) gives

---

[4] When the Israelites leave Egypt suddenly after the death of the Egyptian firstborn, three times the storyteller notes that they go with gifts (Exod 3:20, 11:1, 12:35-36). When slaves are released into freedom, Deut 15:12-18 prescribes a gift. When Cyrus the Persian liberates the Israelite community from their Babylonian captivity, gifts and the plundered Temple treasure precede them home in Ezra 1.

it shelter. His son Eleazar, also priestly-sounding, is consecrated to care for it. And there it dwells for some twenty more years, from which time we lose track of it until David will take it up to Jerusalem. The issue is leadership. Who will care for the ark, past the poor shepherding that let it be captured, mistreated, and then violated as it returns? Who or what sort of leadership is best qualified to tend the relationship between God and people as they return from captivity? The parabolic narrative breaks off as the ark is entrusted to the new man, but we have had our hint. With what sort of leadership will the new community resume its life in the land? Surely not with the same old leadership that has been so thoroughly discredited; perhaps with *ad hoc* caretakers, or with the "requested" son?

How characters talk (4:1–7:17)

Recognizing that events have parabolically and chronotopically referred us into the exile, we need now to listen with a bit more care to how speech proceeds. I have already hinted that the "theology" the first-defeated Israelite elders, beleaguered at Ebenezer, rehearse (4:1) is inadequate. Their precise words are telling: "Why has the LORD put us to rout today before the Philistines? Let us bring the ark of the covenant of the LORD here from Shiloh so that he may come among us and save us from the power of our enemies" (4:3). The assumption is that YHWH was responsible for the defeat and needs to fix it. The elders read the divine hand behind the Philistine slaughter. Missing is any query about the human plane. Their supposing that the relationship with God (so the ark) needs simply to be invoked, to be presumed upon in some automatic way to avert defeat and catastrophe, not only sounds false but is shown to be so. Key and ominous is their literal phraseology: ". . . let us get for ourselves . . . so that it may. . . ." Is the ark to be laid claim to in this way, and is such a presumption of effectiveness justified or not?[5] Again, a moment of reflection will help us review that if victory were so simple the Israelites would have avoided all the misadventures that have plagued them. If you are uncon-

---

[5] It is worth noting that scholars do not agree on the moral valence of the bringing of the ark. James S. Ackerman, "Who Can Stand before YHWH, This Holy God? A Reading of 1 Samuel 1–15," *Prooftexts* 11 (1991) 7, argues that the move is not so clearly portrayed as bad. Lyle Eslinger, *Kingship of God in Crisis: A Close Reading of 1 Samuel 1–12* (Sheffield: Sheffield Academic Press, 1985) 164–66, says we must accept the narrator's assessment of the people's view that God has done it, that God must have forgotten his part of the deal. He also observes, pp.168–69, that no character registers anxiety when the ark and its escorts appear, though he can also say (p.169) that the sound that greets the ark is indeterminate and disputable.

vinced by that suggestion, a glimpse of the ark arriving at the battle attended by Hophni and Phinehas may help: With those two leading the ark
trouble cannot be far away, given what we saw at Shiloh. The narrator carefully juxtaposes the verbal reactions of "our side" and "theirs" as the ark
arrives. Though commentators tend to deride the Philistine "theology" as
poor—"Gods have come into their camp . . ." (4:7), nonetheless there is
little sense of entitlement to victory on the Philistines' part. In fact, making
reference to the deeds of the Israelites' deity, the Philistines realize they
may be in similar danger. Hence they exert themselves "manfully" and
make clear to themselves, to their foe, and presumably to us that the ark
does not save magically and cannot be simplistically equated with God.
Rather good theology!

Again reserving the report of the battle (4:12-22) for a later consideration, we listen in on the Philistine chatter at home (ch. 5); they may seem
clueless at the surface, but their instincts are not so wholly off. Having
given the ark a place of honor in their own shrine, the Philistines learn
quickly and share with us, listening in, that the ark is a happy guest neither
in Dagon's temple nor in any other Philistine city. Though it takes them
seven months to come to such a conclusion, the Philistines are more expe-
ditious in their coping than was the old Eli. Arguably they dishonor the ark
less than did Hophni and Phinehas. The narrator presents the Philistine
leadership struggling verbally, ignorantly but not without sincerity, to
remedy the situation of the ark's capture and exile. In a word, they are no
less wrong about the ark than were the Israelites at 4:3, and presumably with
less information to draw upon. The several colloquies of the Philistines
allow the narrator to rerun the disaster-in-exile chronotope repeatedly, as
the "foreigners" with increasing rapidity recognize the problem.[6] Though
their efforts to return the ark can be dismissed as ritualistic (new cart, un-
broken animals, propitiatory offerings [6:2-9]), not only are their choices
effective enough to get the deed done, but they are similar to the liturgical
action David will institute when he moves the ark later (2 Samuel 6).

The contrast we may have anticipated between Israelite and Philistine
discourse assembled by our storyteller gives way to similarity once we
listen carefully. When they burst into speech the Beth Shemesh community,
like the Philistines, are first eager to receive the ark but then eventually
eager only to be rid of the guest they do not understand well. Like the

---

[6] This similarity of insiders and outsiders—Israelites and Philistines, though we must
note that the Israelites are outsiders while in Philistia and the Philistines insiders—is a point
well discussed by Robert M. Polzin, *Samuel and the Deuteronomist: A Literary Study of the
Deuteronomic History: I Samuel* (San Francisco: Harper & Row, 1989) 55–56.

"foreigners," they send it off to the care of new characters, those with the priestly names. Their question (6:20), "Who is able to stand before the LORD, this holy God?" is reminiscent of the way we may imagine the Philistines asking as they pick up their deity from the place he had fallen, not once but twice. And the Beth Shemeshites' second question, "To whom shall [it] go that we may be rid of [it]?" is quite close to the Philistines' several discussions in 5:7-11, continuing into 6:2-16 until they are satisfied that they have answered their own questions and resolved their own dilemmas.

Samuel reappears at the end of these events, not to care for the literal ark himself but to exhort the people as to their own future. The discourse of the people approaching Samuel in 7:2 hints that the people "lament"[7] after YHWH while the ark is at Kiriath Jearim. Samuel's words, as we follow them now (7:3-14), encourage the people to the "one thing needful," the relationship with God. Samuel says, prophet-like, that God desires only one thing, which is acknowledgment of the divine sovereignty that characterizes YHWH in this book: YHWH alone, with all the heart and service that the people can manage, is what will save them. His language, as scholars correctly maintain, is typical of the viewpoint of the Deuteronomistic editor of the whole narrative, and intones language placed on the lips of leaders from Moses and Joshua to Hezekiah and Josiah: If you are sincere in regard to YHWH, then it must be YHWH alone: only that deity and that deity without consorts, assistants, representation.

The people acknowledge what Samuel has specified, perhaps correcting their theology of 4:3; what sin they confess at 7:6 is not so clear. Though we have not, in this present story, seen worship of what the text calls strange gods, the history has shown it rather frequently in the past, not least in the period of the judges. The pattern of turning toward YHWH when troubles threaten is not new, nor is it bad, depending on sincerity and intention to

---

[7] The problem with the translation is that the word in that precise configuration appears nowhere else in the Hebrew Bible, and hence its denotation is unknowable with precision; the root suggests mourning. Translators, from the earliest who made a Greek translation sometime around the third century B.C.E., calculate that the word means "turn." Context can help, since it appears that the verb indicates something that prompts a change or readiness for it. Commentaries like Ralph W. Klein, *1 Samuel* (Waco: Word Books, 1983) 64–66, give helpful information and their best reasoning on such spots, which are more frequent than many readers suppose. Careful and intentionally poetic translators are instructive as well: Everett Fox, *Give Us A King! Samuel, Saul and David* (New York: Schocken, 1999) 30, chooses "sigh," while Robert Alter, *The David Story: A Translation with Commentary of 1 and 2 Samuel* (New York: W. W. Norton, 1999) 36, opts for "was drawn after," which preserves one of the characteristics of the verb (its reflexive or passive sense) while following a medieval commentator for the meaning. A shift in one of the three root letters (also a relatively frequent situation) yields his choice.

commit. The language about the God-people relationship is more answerable than before, with at least this group acknowledging that they have a role to play; it is not simply God's to save them irrespective of anything. Maintaining appropriate focus on God is not a simple thing, as the tremendous struggles over it attest. Samuel presides at a liturgy where the people recommit themselves, and in an episode reversing the last shocking and devastating battles of Ebenezer (4:1-11), the Philistines are soundly defeated.[8]

God's discourse is thundery but the divine hand effective. The relationship seems back on track, if "back" is the word. That the victory is a reward for the ceremony is not articulated by Samuel or the narrator, and we need to be leery of making such a link too tight. Samuel surely appreciates the people's sentiment and God's participation in victory, and he marks out a memorial of God's assistance: Ebenezer is literally a stone of help (7:12). But his "thus far the LORD has helped us" is not an expression of entitlement. God's answerability gets some nuance here, if we are alert for it. That God was responsible for the "exile" is not a conclusion toward which we need rush. We may think all will go forward smoothly for a time, especially as we review Samuel's professional credentials.

The falling of the mighty (4:12-22)

But there remains a piece of the story we have not yet discussed: the report of the initial catastrophes of Ebenezer back to the Shiloh shrine (4:12-22). Though still partaking in the genres of parable or riddle, it can also be seen to work as a figure called *mise-en-abyme*.[9] Robert Polzin,

---

[8] The narrator's indication that the Philistine problem is wholly solved for all time (7:13-14), clearly not the case, is again a cue to the riddling genre.

[9] The most-quoted source for this small genre is Lucien Dällenbach, *The Mirror in the Text,* translated by Jeremy Whiteley with Emma Hughes (Cambridge: Polity Press, 1989). To summarize a topic that needs, in his view, both precision and some scope for its occurrences: Dällenbach links the expression first to heraldry, where the design of a whole shield is found emblazoned in the middle of the shield (in the "abyss/*abyme*"), and then to the sort of refractions possible with mirrors. Thus the *mise-en-abyme* is a structure by which the whole of a narrative is refracted in a moment of it, where some key moment is represented to a character (and reader) in a way available for insight and transformation. It is a refraction, recognizable but repositioned, a replica in smaller scale and from a different perspective, compressed but discernible. Here the sense is that Eli's collapse mirrors the whole dynamic of his "reign," possibly the whole self-destructiveness of monarchy. Polzin uses the expression "story within a story" (e.g., of ch. 17) to point to the same general thing (p. 170). See Adele Berlin, *Poetics and Interpretation of Biblical Narrative* (Sheffield: Almond Press, 1983) 68–70, for excellent observations regarding viewpoint, particularly how we are given blind Eli's angle here.

whose insights have guided us substantially so far, has discussed brilliantly the capacity of this short scene to recapitulate the story of collapsing monarchy of which it is a minor detail.[10] The scene's perspective is partially that of the old priest Eli, seated and awaiting information, presumably since the ark has departed. The narrator tells us that Eli's heart fears for the ark, tardily, we may think; no other object of concern is named specifically. Though the messenger, a Benjaminite, is described for us as to physical appearance, Eli's blindness deprives him of that information. In fact, in the riddling language to which I hope you are becoming accustomed, his blindness is not a great surprise, since we have seen him miss-see and overlook throughout the story so far. That we see and Eli hears gives us a doubled angle. That the battle has been lost we know already, and we read it afresh in the demeanor of the runner, whose torn clothing and muddy appearance are signs not only of defeat but of ritual mourning. The messenger is thus a picture of the news he is about to impart. Eli's sightless watching cannot pick that up, so the marked messenger and the blind watchman are for readers. The narrator skillfully directs our attention again to the question of inept, failed leadership.

What Eli cannot read directly he picks up indirectly, as the messenger occasions an uproar on the part of the place. Though Eli presumably may guess that the news cannot be good, he has not been characterized as a very good listener either, and he demands to have the news told him. "What is this uproar?" (4:14). In between his question and its response (information we already know), the narrator tells us of the old man's age and eyesight. Then comes the direct discourse:

> The man said to Eli, "I have just come from the battle; I fled from the battle today." He said, "How did it go, my son?" The messenger replied, "Israel has fled before the Philistines, and there has also been a great slaughter among the troops; your two sons also, Hophni and Phinehas, are dead, and the ark of God has been captured." When he mentioned the ark of God, Eli fell over backward from his seat by the side of the gate; and his neck was broken and he died, for he was an old man, and heavy. He had judged Israel for forty years (4:16-18).

We have been given a great deal of crucial information. As I have already suggested, the narrator sees to it that our shock is not the news of the defeat, the capture of the ark. We learn most by attending not to the content but to the manner of the report. The narrator, again subverting realism, has

---

[10] Polzin, *Samuel and the Deuteronomist* ch. 2, especially 55–60.

the town learn of the news before Eli does, even though he is attentive at the city gate and can scarcely be imagined not to intercept a newcomer entering the gates. The messenger overlooks blind Eli, who does not see his embodied message. Failed leadership is once again underscored. Eli's slowness or reluctance to construe the significance of what he hears in the reaction of the city gives us a chance to watch him closely. He calls the messenger "my son," perhaps conventional for an old man to a young warrior; but in this case it recalls his address to the young Samuel in 3:16, to his own two in 2:24. That the messenger is a Benjaminite, unnamed, gives the careful-reading and resourceful rabbis of later centuries the space to identify him as the young Saul. In our riddling mode the runner's identity is shrewdly observed. It helps us make the transition from the "old sons" of Eli, including the much-asked Samuel, to the new son Saul, whom we will be meeting shortly.[11]

When Eli hears—not of the defeat of the people, not of the death of his sons (which we, with him, have been awaiting since 2:34), but of the exile of the ark—he falls over backwards, toppled by his own weight and age. As Polzin says, "If chapters 1–7 form an overture to the entire monarchic history, the picture in 4:18 of Eli falling backward off his throne to his death is this overture's central event, the Deuteronomist's view of kingship in a nutshell. Eli represents all the burden and doom that kingship brought Israel."[12] Hannah's words about the high and the low (2:7-8) receive fresh significance, as the old man topples from his place of honor. We find out, for the first time, that Eli is not simply a priest but also a judge, the first we have heard mentioned since the death of the notorious Samson (Judges 13–16), who fought Philistines intermittently, but on the whole ineffectually. The destructive events of Judges 17–21 are hence laid, if indirectly, at the feet of Eli, are implied to have occurred on his watch—the watch of a blind man.[13] But attentive reading will not miss this final slur on Elide leadership.

The final scene of chapter 4 picks up as well on the prophecy of the man of God from chapter 2 and on the exilic chronotope. The narrator, having shown us the reaction of Eli to news of the ark's exile, next recounts the reaction of his daughter-in-law to both the capture of the ark and the

[11] Eli has also used (4:13-14) the word *hgd,* which is the word for "relate" or "make known" and will set up for an extended wordplay on the word *nagid* or "designated leaders."

[12] Polzin, *Samuel and the Deuteronomist* 64.

[13] Jobling, *1 Samuel* ch. 3 discusses the relationship between the end of the story told in Judges and the opening chapters of 1 Samuel. Whether he is correct in all his surmises is less important than that we consider the possibilities he has opened up by his careful comments.

demise of Eli. Pregnant and about to bear, she stoops to give birth, drawing our attention once again to the chronotope of falling, of untimely exile. The child's birth is early and the mother's death premature. The discourse of the women attending her would soothe her, telling her that she has borne a son, helping us remark both her similarity and difference from Hannah. This new mother's response is difficult to construe, for the narrator says that she did not answer or give heed, leaving ambiguous whether or not the words of those attending her penetrate perceptively her awareness or not.[14] In either case she comments, also somewhat ambiguously, in the small genre of naming her child. This son was not asked in our hearing but receives a question to mark him—and to draw our attention to the main issue of the section: Ichabod translates as "where the glory?" a tag with which the narrator assists us to link the vanishing of the ark of God to the deaths of her male kin.[15] This mother's last words are her own answer to the question that names her child: "The glory has departed from Israel, for the ark of God has been captured" (4:22).

Conclusions

While listening to the riddle of the ark's journey and a bit beyond it we have moved toward a number of conclusions that we can summarize for reflection. First, both the falling of Eli and the birth of the immediately-orphaned Ichabod serve purposes far beyond their obvious content. The dynasty of Eli sustains a deathblow, with not only the sons but the father dying on the same day. A provocatively-named scion survives, though we will meet not him but his offspring in the story ahead. The Shiloh scene underscores not only the direct promises of the divine voice (the man of God's to Eli [2:27-36] and God's to Samuel [3:11-14]) about the dispossession of the Elides from their position but also the words of Hannah (2:1-10) that trace reversals: high to low, barren to fertile; but the dynamic of which she speaks implies the possibility of further reversal as well. This report to Shiloh brings the opening scene set there full circle as the house of Eli dwindles to one, whose status is unclear.

---

[14] P. Kyle McCarter, *1 Samuel. A New Translation with Introduction and Commentary* (Garden City, N.Y.: Doubleday, 1980) 115, alerts us to the possibilities that either she is so despondent as to be oblivious of efforts to console her, or the consolers have misconstrued her demeanor. The exact nuance is undecidable, one of the many ways in which this narrative assures us of spaciousness for careful reading.

[15] As noted above, the same three consonants manage "glory" and "heavy."

Second, we may reflect on the forty-five or so verses spent on the adventures of the ark, first in a foreign land but also in its own territory. This narrative helps direct our attention ahead in space and time, chronotopically. As we envision the much later community of exiles, urged to return to Judah perhaps by the golden voice of Second Isaiah or chivvied by the stern language of the priest-and-prophet Ezekiel, we can get a sense of that group's dilemma. Though the biblical storyline makes it clear that there is no king crowned after the last several who became casualties of the Babylonians in one way or another, to end the monarchy after hundreds of years cannot have been a simple matter. Practicalities and even politics aside (which they surely were not!), the monarchy was heavily tangled with the notion of God's special care for the people Israel. The fact that a strong desire for an anointed leader will outlast the experience of crowned heads by hundreds of years attests to the strength of the image of a leader anointed by God. The later Christian belief that Jesus of Nazareth claimed that role signally is only one of the later manifestations of the Jewish longing for an anointed hero.

The biblical texts trace only sketchily the process of return from Babylon. They hint that one Sheshbazzar, grandson to the old king-in-exile Jehoiachin, is given the task of returning the plundered temple vessels to Jerusalem. The earliest of the post-exilic texts indicate a doubled leadership, priestly and royal, the latter carried briefly by Zerubbabel after his uncle Sheshbazzar drops out. The return to the old site of Judah (now called Yehud) and the struggle to cope with various challenges are related; all of them call for leadership and show tension among the locals as the exiles return. Historian Diana Edelman has pointed out that certain genealogies in Chronicles suggest the sixth-century presence of Saul descendants in the neighborhood who contest the Davidic claims and give our "ancient" stories fresh relevance.[16] We, and surely the intended audience of this work, have to feel somewhat caught between the intense desire for a "son," signaled by the asking that we saw generate the young Samuel, and the finality of the toppling of the old dynast Eli, whose family has so debased

---

[16] For detail consult Tamara Eskenazi, *In An Age of Prose: A Literary Approach to Ezra and Nehemiah* (Atlanta: Scholars, 1988) stating on pp. 37–94 and succinctly on p. 175 her case for a plausible alternative to both kingly and "judge-ly" leadership; see also Sara Japhet, "Sheshbazzar and Zerubbabel: Against the Background of the Historical and Religious Tendencies of Ezra-Nehemiah," *ZAW* 95 (1983) 218–29. I am appreciative of the early circulation of a forthcoming article by Diana Edelman, "Did Saulide-Davidic Rivalry Resurface in Early Persian Yehud?" in M. P. Graham and J. A. Dearman, eds., *The Land That I Will Show You: Essays in the History and Archaeology of the Ancient Near East in Honor of J. Maxwell Miller.* JSOTSup 343 (Sheffield: Sheffield Academic Press, 2001) 70–92.

its role. The events of chapters 4–7, tracing the ark out of the land and back in, coming to rest but not being received appropriately by the local population until a new man is selected to care for it, make the question and the answer clear, it seems to me. Shall the community coalesce under old—Elide—leadership, the same group that caused the debacles in the first place? In no way! With survivor sons? But they are discredited. With dynastic leadership at all? Insofar as Eli's chair is both royal and priestly, the answer once again seems clear. And yet we have not met the first king yet, so the story remains to be told.

A third concluding point leads us back to Bakhtin's answerability. The "one thing needful" is for a leader to shepherd well the bond between God and people. Insofar as the ark is a symbol of that relationship—makes manifest the commitment of YHWH to the people chosen and their responsive worship and culture—the leadership has not only failed but abused its task. The Elides bring the ark to the occasion of its exile and that catastrophe wipes them out, except for a newborn. The general populace has acknowledged their struggle to remain faithful to YHWH, however much they may wish to do so, especially as trouble looms. As the ark returns, a split leadership emerges, royal (in the person of Samuel) and priestly (Eleazar mustered on the spot but retiring into seclusion with the ark). Samuel, however, is aging and will shortly turn out to have only a pair of malfeasant sons to follow him (8:1-3). If the people seem to be guessing badly what God desires of them (4:3, 6:20), it is also evident that God does not help them much here. Clearer about what is wrong than about what is right, God seems to communicate in negative space, failing to meet the unreal expectations heaped upon the ark by those who speak of it and manage it, whether at Ebenezer, Philistia, or Beth Shemesh. A thundery growl is the clearest divine communication (7:10); that the Philistines suffer a big defeat in one battle does not signify too clearly if we peek around the story's corner, since they have additional thunder of their own to let loose. What *is* expected from characters in this narrative? The story of the first king is only now about to start in plain(er) talk. Prior to the curtain's rising in 1 Samuel 8 we have been entertained by the performers while the house lights are still up. But the view from the end of chapter 7—or perhaps from the first three verses of chapter 8—makes a similar circle and dumps us abruptly back into reality. Though the answer to the asking of sons seems negative, we will view it again and aim to understand its communication more fully and perhaps more personally for ourselves.

CHAPTER THREE

Request for a King (1 Samuel 8–12)

"The artist's struggle to achieve a determinate and stable image of
the hero is to a large degree his struggle with himself."

Mikhail Bakhtin, "Author and Hero"

Who asks for King Saul, requests Saul for king? Who is—who are—
responsible, answerable, for (his) kingship in Israel? How is the story recounted, and with what effect? Why is it told in such particular detail?
How are we to read it well? Though historians are keen to get at the historical moments beneath this moment, and I join them in wishing such a thing
more possible than I hold it to be, our aim will be rather to focus upon Saul
as a representation. We have, in a certain sense, left the parable genre,
though our story continues to construct a riddle for its readers. In this long
and detailed section of the story we will restrict ourselves to genre considerations and meet the events narrated here by following the characters as they
step from question to question, attending to the specificity of each query
but also to the spaciousness for our interpretation that questions invite. And
since the questions arise from the discourse of characters, we will once
again be paying careful attention to how their speech proceeds.

If our concept of answerability appeared to get short shrift in the last
chapter, it will dominate here, as we visit this fateful moment of a request
and its granting. Since our riddling preview has already made tangible the
disaster of dynastic sons we may think it a foregone conclusion that monarchy
is wrong. But our storyteller is far more subtle than that. What he relates is
that it *did not* go well, since such was likely his conclusion from sifting his

evidence and presumably the point he is eager to underscore. But it *need not* have gone badly, was not inherently a doomed project. How and why it failed is the story to be explored now: first for the original exilic community upon whom we have focused so far, and second for a wider set of human beings who may gain insight from this complex portrait of the askers and the asked in Israel. Since the problem of whether to have kings or not is not the current concern of contemporary readers—though leadership crises are not absent from our lives, at many levels—I will spend more energy on the more transferrable aspects of the moral portraiture here. The epigraph that opens this chapter suggests that all authoring, including the constructions made by careful readers, is to some extent self-portraiture. That is, our reading is part of the authoring of the story. As we come to know this character Saul we are asked to "answer" for the traits we discern in him, especially as he interacts with God.

"Support beams" of the section

If you have ever watched a house take shape from the foundations up through the furnishing stage you will likely recall that certain decisions made early in the project (e.g., which walls will bear weight, where plumbing will be placed) radically affect all aspects of the living space without necessarily drawing a lot of attention to themselves. I think something similar pertains here. Before we turn to the text let me make visible some of the structure, the "support beams" for my own reading of the request for a king. The main aim here is to facilitate your capacity to disagree, to develop your own architecture, as you probe the story more deeply.

First, and most important, I view the manner of asking to be defective. Israel asks for a king over God's head, so to speak, as though God were irrelevant to the leadership crisis. Second, as the asking goes forward there are numerous occasions to back off, but it never happens; in fact, as the bonds holding the king in place become tangled they are reinforced. Third, the enterprise is from start to finish a team effort. Participating like climbers roped together are three individuals crucially involved (Samuel, Saul, and God), a group (Israel) and numerous "bit players," the highly influential narrator, and our readerly selves. A good deal of what transpires is characters at cross-purposes, underspeaking, talking past each other. If we were their group facilitator we would have our work cut out for us! Fourth, no character is malevolent; there is no equivalent of Hophni and Phinehas in this part of the story, which makes diagnosing the problem more challenging. Fifth, we need to recall that the story takes shape under the constraint of what has already happened in history rather than as a plan for the future.

The story to be told includes kings, and that the monarchy was a disaster is the story to be told. As we look now in more detail I hope you will evaluate and customize—or revise—these "support beams" of mine as you construct your own reading.

Exposition of the text

Having said that we will focus primarily on the character questions that comprise the king's requesting, we need to start with the moment of asking, which does not come in technical question form but is obviously central (ch. 8). The narrator has just completed the story of failed sons, and our next information is that Samuel sets *his* two renegade offspring in positions of leadership. The elders of the community appear before him and speak somewhat directly about the problem: You are old, your sons are crooks, they say; we need a king to rule us, as other nations have. Samuel brings his version of this request, presumably a version of what we witnessed, before God. God's reaction seems best characterized as shock and hurt, deep distress, feeling the request as a rejection that falls into a pattern of previous rejections. Do as they say, God concedes—but tell them what it will be like to have a king. And leaving God to brood, Samuel returns to the elders' gathering and relates what it will be like without, so far as we hear, mentioning that God is grieved and has taken the request as a rejection.[1]

Though some scholars think the reality check Samuel recites in 8:10-18 is tantamount to a negative reply from the deity, that is not really so clear. One way to view those words is that the king will not work alone and must requisition what he needs to get the job done: personnel, goods, authority. Whether this first list of what the king will claim is exorbitant need not detain us here, since we can watch how the man chosen will manage his needs. A second point frequently raised is that to ask for a human king affronts the divine incumbent. That argument seems abstract to me, since the Bible abounds with human intermediaries who are necessary in human culture: judges, priests, prophets all struggle prominently to specify what God wants.[2] We do not hear Samuel stress God's particular appraisal of the

---

[1] This move seems to me similar to the community's bringing the ark onto the scene when they are in trouble, as though it of itself can be a savior. David M. Gunn, *The Fate of King Saul: An Interpretation of a Biblical Story* (Sheffield: JSOT Press, 1980) 60, notes that God offers no alternative; Diana V. Edelman, *King Saul in the Historiography of Judah* (Sheffield: Sheffield Academic Press, 1991) 38–39, wonders how the elders anticipated Samuel to respond.

[2] Edelman, *Saul* 36–39, remarks that all ancient Near Eastern kings will be regents for their deities, all kingship theocratic.

request for a king to the elders. But the people seem scarcely to listen to the warning and say at the end, "No![3] But we are determined to have a king over us so that we also may be like other nations, and that our king may govern us and go out before us and fight our battles" (8:19-20). Again God agrees. Some questions: Has Samuel heard the elders' comments about his age and sons? Has he been adequate in his intermediation task? Have the people been insightful enough about the nature of the problem, which after all includes their own shortcomings as well as Samuel's? Are their already-shaking heads ominous? Has God been sufficiently clear, or perhaps too sensitive? too permissive? Is the project of kingship off to a good start, do you think?[4]

Our central character enters the story unobtrusively. When finally we meet the young man from Benjamin, assigned by his father to search for lost animals through regions linked paronomasially to his name (Shalishah, Shaalim [9:1-4]), it may seem a letdown. Pleasant and pliable, he does as he is asked until he fails, at which point he suggests to his servant-companion that they return home lest the father's anxiety over lost animals give way to concern over a lost son. Saul's first spoken words are worth quoting: "Let us turn back . . ." (9:5). It is his servant who prevails upon Saul to seek assistance from the man of God, resident in the town they are near. Saul, agreeable, voices the first question for us to examine: "But if we go, what can we bring the man? For the bread in our sacks is gone, and there is no present to bring the man of God. What have we?" (9:7). The question is less important for its practical referent than for its discourse, since the Hebrew syllables ask not only what I have just quoted but say as well, "What is a prophet to the man?" It is an excellent (if enigmatic) and agenda-setting question in this story of Saul and Samuel, king and prophet. It will get considerably more play than the simpler query about fees, which the servant manages deftly by producing some small change.

As the two men proceed toward the town and meet young women coming to draw water, they inquire, "Is the seer here?" (9:11). Again we look beyond the obvious. The men's question gives these otherwise minor characters an opportunity to swell the chorus of voices urging Saul to his

---

[3] Peter D. Miscall, *1 Samuel: A Literary Reading* (Bloomington: Indiana University Press, 1986) 50, asks what they are negating. My sense of the scene is that, as Samuel speaks, heads shake, indicating that there is no openness to the position the prophet represents, perhaps directing us to Deut 18:19 where the consequences of not heeding a prophet are related.

[4] For good conversation on some of these points consult Robert M. Polzin, *Samuel and the Deuteronomist: A Literary Study of the Deuteronomic History: I Samuel* (San Francisco: Harper & Row, 1989) ch. 3.

destiny.[5] The men's question also underlines the fact that the two seekers do not know whom they are approaching, as in fact theoretically neither do we.

By means of an important flashback we watch the "seer," who turns out to be none other than the prophet Samuel, tapped on the shoulder by God and told to anticipate meeting YHWH's choice. We are given the deity's expectation of what the king is to do: save the people from the Philistines (9:15-16). A day later, as Samuel spots Saul, the "seer" is given a second divine nudge: here he is, God indicates (9:17). Beyond a doubt it is Saul that God chooses to be ruler. Incidentally, though my contention is that the people have overlooked God in coping with their worries, and though Samuel has threatened that when they call later God will not respond (8:20), here God shows a divine sensitivity to human need, however imperfectly voiced: *I* have heard it, God says, I *have* heard (9:16). What we lack most notably is some sense of criteria for God's choice. Some of you may feel that Saul is set up by God, chosen to fail. Each of us will find it telling to examine our own authoring here and to listen carefully also as others fill in what they hear from this deeply ambiguous text. How is God participating in the project? Diverse readings of those in our company help us recognize our own assumptions, of which the question of divine benevolence or malevolence is fundamental. In the meantime Saul once again inquires the way to the seer's house, this time unknowingly addressing the prophet seer himself (9:18). The discrepancy in their knowledge and viewpoints makes the scene work powerfully. Samuel knows Saul is God's choice for king, whatever other data he may lack, but Saul has not recognized the man who will anoint him nor, we must note, does he get clear information about it for some time.[6]

We move from these superficially simple though quite pregnant questions now to something more visibly complex. Reassuring Saul (if that is the likely effect) that the lost animals are already found, the "local seer" asks, "And on whom is all Israel's desire fixed, if not on you and on all your ancestral house?" (9:20).[7] Saul's rejoinder is to self-deprecate,[8] asking,

---

[5] Shimon Bar-Efrat, *Narrative Art in the Bible* (Sheffield: Almond Press, 1989) 97, points out that the utterance of the young women suggests a medley of voices answering rather than a single, clear response from a knowledgeable representative.

[6] Scholars worry considerably over the likelihood of Samuel's apparent anonymity here. But insofar as we are watching an artistic representation rather than trying to uncover facticity, it works.

[7] This rather open-ended query is so enigmatic that scholars interpret it quite diversely. Lyle Eslinger, *Kingship of God in Crisis: A Close Reading of 1 Samuel 1–12* (Sheffield: Sheffield Academic Press, 1985) 312, notes helpfully that it may be framed not for Saul but for readers.

[8] For a good discussion of some presumed social circumstances under which such a reply is called for see Philip Esler, "The Madness of Saul: A Cultural Reading of 1 Samuel

"Why have you spoken to me in this way?" (9:21). Saul's question keys us to the gap between the two men. The point of it is not so much its specific reference (which remains somewhat opaque) but its undertow of the desire of all Israel for something that Saul now represents. Many hands propel Saul toward the kingship: the elders who have insisted on a king against practical advice, the father who sends his son out on a quest for strayed animals, the servant who prevents his going back home, the young women who reassure him he is headed correctly, God who has spoken clearly to the prophet, and Samuel himself. Saul's speech, we must now begin to notice, is tentative in a variety of ways, making a contrast with the insistence of many others.

But whether Saul is eager or not, a sacrifice proceeds with Samuel presiding and the young man of Benjamin as an honored guest. Next morning he is privately though clearly made ruler/*nagid*[9] over YHWH's people, kissed, addressed, anointed by the prophet. And he is addressed with a question (which has been made an assertion in English translations): "Has not YHWH anointed you *nagid* over his inheritance?" (10:1, author's translation). Though we may have occasion to doubt it as things develop, the question reinforces yet again the divine participation in this action. Samuel is the agent, but God is the one who has made the selection. As the two men reverse their paths, which are shortly to diverge, Samuel speaks to Saul of a series of signs that will attend the young man's return, presumably to reassure him of Samuel's reliability. Buried in the first of them is a query emerging from the shadowy Kish, father of Saul: "What shall I do about my son?" (10:2). Though we never see a worried father articulating such a question, in this story so studded with paternal and filial interaction it is a poignant and multivalent question. While the absent Kish cannot know it, there is nothing he can do to prevent what lies ahead, as Saul falls heir to an inheritance other than that of his father. As Samuel had said when warning the elders of the cost of kingship, sons are taken, and Kish's son is first of them. Saul, tellingly, makes no response to either of these anticipated questions.

8-31," in J. Cheryl Exum and Stephen D. Moore, eds., *Biblical Studies/Cultural Studies* (Sheffield: Sheffield Academic Press, 1998) 220–62, and Hugh S. Pyper, *David as Reader: 2 Samuel 12:1-15 and the Poetics of Fatherhood* (Leiden: E. J. Brill, 1996) 175, who reminds us that Saul will later sneer at David's humble lineage. What seems more relevant to me is to recognize that Saul draws himself small.

[9] Scholars are in general agreement that the word means a king-designate; my point is that additionally it is a word play, drawing its life from its root letters *hgd,* which suggest the sense of making something known. The pun snakes throughout the book of 1 Samuel (e.g., in this section at 8:9; 9:6, 8, 16, 18, 19; 10:1, 15, 16), not always obvious in English transla-

The tone shifts as we watch the signs—of which there seem to be four—move into actuality (10:1-8). For as the new king turns to go, God gives him a new heart; he soon meets a band of prophets, is rushed by the *ruaḥ* (spirit or breath) of God, and acts-the-prophet with them. Once again it would be helpful to know exactly what he did, but we must "follow the questions," which are several here as bystanders speculate: "'What has come over the son of Kish? Is Saul also among the prophets? . . . 'And who is their father?' . . . Therefore it became a proverb, 'Is Saul also among the prophets?'" (10:9-13).[10] The clearest thing we can mark here is the surprise of those who see the Saul they had known. They register surprise at the company he is keeping as well as his participation in a group of prophets. Though the tone is difficult to assess, it seems to me that the surprise is not approval. The question "Who is their father?" refers, in all likelihood, to the leader of such a band of men. But in our story the language underlines again the persistent motif of fathers and sons. These bystanders, then, allow us by their reaction to see something unusual: Saul with the prophets, Saul acting like a prophet.[11] The fourth sign Samuel has given Saul—that Saul is to go to Gilgal and await Samuel who will come and sacrifice and tell him what to do (10:8)—we must await to see unfold in our next chapter.

When he returns home Saul is met not by an anxious father but by a curious uncle, who quizzes him about his adventures (10:14-16). "Where did you go?" he asks. And we listen to Saul answer minimally, not lying but surely not making everything known. In so short an episode we do not get much, but we do sense the uneasiness of Saul about sharing even within his own family what has happened. And, indeed, the episode reminds us that no one except Samuel, Saul, and YHWH know that the king has been selected, as in law needs to occur.[12] So Samuel convenes the tribes

tion. See P. Kyle McCarter, *1 Samuel. A New Translation with Introduction and Commentary* (Garden City, N. Y.: Doubleday, 1980) 176–79 and 186–87, for useful comment.

[10] Everett Fox, *Give Us A King! Samuel, Saul and David* (New York: Schocken, 1999) 34, usefully characterizes Saul as not able to handle YHWH's spirit well, to which I would add that the divine party does not deal very effectively with Saul either!

[11] Polzin maintains and develops a case that the king's mixing a prophetic role into his "job description" is one of the most fundamental wrongs established throughout the long story. I am disinclined to give it so much weight (having another candidate for the basic flaw), but what Polzin has convinced me of is a tag on the problem of how the king and the prophet will interact, surely a key issue in the long story of prophets and kings that stretches hundreds of years ahead.

[12] Deut 17:14-20 is the legislation that prescribes the choice of the king. In the Law such a request is condoned, with the limitation that the choice is to be God's; the king will be kin, not foreigner, and must eschew certain behaviors. The only specific task in his "job description"

and the choice of the king is made clear by lots, the presumption being that the realm of the divine controls the falling of the lots (10:17-20). Only now, and almost incidentally, does the prophet make explicit that God had felt the request as a rejection but is prepared to accede to it nonetheless. The Benjamin tribe is indicated by lots and then the appropriate lineage and finally the man himself. Saul, meanwhile, has disappeared, and so once again he must be sought—asked, and from God: "Did the man come here?" people press to learn (10:22).[13]

The point is not so much to discuss the psychology of the king—though I think we are getting a picture of reluctance—but to notice that God is unswervingly clear about the identity of the divine choice. Once God has conceded that there will be a king (so at 8:7, 9, 22; 9:15-17; 10:1), it is clearly to be Saul, first shown in this passage by lot and then as God reveals Saul's hiding place, making the man all the more visible for his effort to hide. It is at this moment that the narrator characterizes the newly anointed man as tall—head and shoulders above all the people. And to insure that we see it the prophet Samuel asks, "Do you see the one whom the LORD has chosen? There is no one like him among all the people" (10:24). Is this a good sign, the tallness of this Benjaminite?[14] In the chronotope (linked time/space) of the Deuteronomistic History the tall are prone to topple, as we have seen and heard. But perhaps it can work well. As if to assist the likelihood that it will, Samuel reiterates the rights and duties of the king in the hearing of the people and records them in a document laid up before God (10:25). If this is a reference to the procedure in Deut 17:18-20, in fact the only charge that the Law specifically gives the king, then we must observe that it has been done. Or has it been? Has the king made himself a copy of the Law that is his now to understand so that it can work well to deepen the relatedness between God and people, the "one thing needful" we have seen before? Or has the prophet done it for him and placed the

---

is the copying and reflection upon "this law," so that his leadership may lengthen the abiding of the community of Israel in God's land.

[13] The question is more literally rendered by Fox, *Give Us A King!* 48: "Has any other man come here?" and by Robert Alter, *The David Story: A Translation with Commentary of 1 and 2 Samuel* (New York: W. W. Norton & Company, 1999) 58: "Has a man come [again] here?"

[14] In the last episode of the book of Judges that precedes 1 Samuel, the tribe of Benjamin has most unpleasantly been implicated in a civil war resulting in the slaughter of several hundred thousand of Israel (if we total the information of Judg 20:21, 25, 35, 44, 46, and 21:11). At the personal level we could say it has nothing to do with this individual young man of Benjamin. But structurally, if we are intuiting a question about the viability of royal rule it is sobering and admonitory.

copy with God instead of with the king? The matter is undecidable, but we will not see Saul consulting any such document throughout his reign.

But the people have acclaimed Saul as king (10:24). Clearly most, though not all, approve. For once the public ceremony is over and all have departed for home, some ne'er-do-wells (characterized with the same epithet as was used for Eli's misreading of Hannah-at-prayer and for Hophni and Phinehas [1:16; 2:12]) ask, "How can this man save us?" (10:27). Once again the question is valuable for us. Some resist the asking of Saul to rule but nothing is done, even by the king himself, who, the narrator hints, knows of the grumbled queries. And the "saving" question makes fresh in our minds the task that has woven its way through the descriptions of the king. He is consistently cast in the role of rescuing the people (implied in 8:11-12, clear in 8:20; 9:16; 10:1). And such a rescue, not too surprisingly, is the next thing we see. When the people of Jabesh in Gilead (across the Jordan River to the north of Saul's own region) are threatened by a perennial East-Jordan dwelling foe called the Ammonites they make an appeal for help. Though they do not appeal to Saul directly, when he hears of the distress he inquires as to the cause: "What is the matter with the people, that they are weeping?" (11:5). As soon as he hears, God's spirit rushes him into action and he organizes their effective deliverance. Rallying the Israelite tribes in a way we will not see again from Saul, sending back the people of Jabesh with a promise of assistance, he manages the affair so well that no two Ammonites are left together (11:11). Vintage saving.[15]

The text shifts back, now, to take up the resistance to the new king that closed the public anointing ceremony; "the people" ask Saul: "Who is it that said, 'Shall Saul reign over us?' Give them to us that we may put them to death" (11:12). Once again the Hebrew, consisting of three words —Saul / will or does rule / over us—is ambiguous, and may be read as an assertion or as a question.[16] But Saul demurs. Who are the people who question the choice of Saul, and what are their reasons? We do not get the

---

[15] Many of those who work with this material sense that it has been edited or redacted to a new whole from disparate sources, with the original roots still dangling visibly. One topic raised in relation to the story of ch. 11 is to ask whether Saul is drawn like a (pre-monarchic) judge (a case made by Miscall, *1 Samuel* 66–67) or like a king (see Jan P. Fokkelman, *Narrative Art and Poetry in the Books of Samuel: Volume IV: Vow and Desire* [Assen, The Netherlands: Van Gorcum, 1993] 465–77). I am avoiding the "layering of sources" question but agree from my own angle that the Jabesh Gilead story feels very different from every other story of Saul, suggesting that it is a likely refugee from some other realm.

[16] Commentators wonder if a negative fell out and speculate as to the tone. Hebrew does not use quotation or question marks, nor is it laden with particles to help us know for certain how the words interrelate.

opportunity to hear and so are left to wonder on our own. Why has Saul bypassed their question, seemed reluctant to air the matter, and what are possible effects of that choice of his? It is another moment, perhaps, when kingship might have been reversed. Instead we see it made more firm than before. Samuel speaks up and urges that the kingship be renewed, and so it is, at Gilgal: The people make Saul king before YHWH, with Samuel's support, in a cultic setting. All Israel rejoices, the narrator sums up (11:14-15) —the king included, we may ask?

Our last questions nestle in a final chapter of our consideration (ch. 12) that will remind us, I think, of chapter 7, where Samuel rallied the people who came to him "mourning" after God and managed their repentance of whatever had happened in regard to false gods. Though scholars can make a good case for the disjunction between this present scene and the events of requesting the king (ch. 8), at least the last hand to shape the material seems to have made a logical progression from Saul's saving of Jabesh to the renewal of kingship and finally to this speech of Samuel's. It is that logic we will follow. The long chapter also serves as the bookend to the assembly that opened this story of royal asking. There the elders confronted Samuel with his old age and the inadequacy of his two sons, bringing to the fore again the endemic leadership deficiency.

Samuel begins here with a claim that he and his sons have done well, his staccato questions of 12:1-5 reintoning some of his language of 8:11-19 to insist upon his integrity. But in the meantime a king is in place, also not without episode and surely not without uncertainty. So what does the prophet have in mind as he addresses the community at Gilgal, after (as the narrative now reads) the renewal of the kingship? Samuel's defensiveness can perhaps be sensed as he presents his list of short questions to the people about his own leadership: "'Whom have I defrauded?'" he asks, presenting a checklist of animals he has not stolen, hands from whom he has not taken bribes, and the like. No one present argues with him, and indeed his questions seem beside the point. The leadership problems faced by the community are not a product of Samuel's personal dishonesty; the problem is structural, longitudinal, a point made afresh when the old prophet prefaces his list of queries with his reference to his two sons. Once again the matter is on the table before us: how are sons the solution, how the problem?

Though Samuel moves, finally now, to develop the case that the people ought not to have disregarded God in their request for a human king (12:6-12), and though the people acknowledge at 12:10 and later at 12:19 the pattern of rejection God had made to Samuel in 8:7-9, the prophet shifts unexpectedly from "memory lane" to insist that all is not lost. What

Samuel proposes is exactly the same point we have seen previously. This long speech distills his statements of 12:14-15 and 20-25: Insofar as the king, whom the people have asked and received, brings about mutual, functioning fidelity between God and themselves it will be well for all of them; if not, they may anticipate being swept away, king and people.[17] The question, as the first and epitomic king is selected, is: can Saul be such a leader? The answer, coded into the narrative, is that sons go bad, that the tall fall; the one who is asked demurs and is repudiated. Abstractly it need not be so, but that is the fact of it. The very evidence Samuel sees fit to select for his long (by Bible standards!) speech of infidelities does not conduce to optimism about the future. The people make no response to this stark choice Samuel has offered. Ringing in our ear are his words ". . . you shall be swept away, both you and your king" (12:25).

Concluding questions

Having negotiated the complex and tangled discourse, the series of ambiguous queries that constructs first the kingship and then the king, we must ask who can answer for this selection. Will the people be able to take responsibility for their part, they who seem to lack crucial information about God's views as the story develops and receive it too late to act upon it? Will Samuel be answerable for the man he has anointed, this prophet somewhat out of step with those between whom he shuttles? Has his slowness to disclose fully the reaction of God thwarted the kingship project? Has his tendency to override, perhaps manipulate the people been effective so far? And has God done well to feel rejection so strongly, to listen in to what was not asked specifically of the divine self? Has the selection of the tall man been a propitious one? Has God backed off a bit from this project?

What sense can we make, do you make of Saul's prominent hesitation to be king, his apparent squeamishness about handling both approbation and opposition? Is there any sense in which Saul seems to have been set up by all of these askers? Will he be able to take responsibility well for his new position, to be *nagid* in both senses of the word: designated leader, embodiment of a riddle to be communicated? Saul speaks ten times in this section (9:5, 7, 10, 11, 18, 21; 10:16; 11:5, 7, 13). His words tend to cancel out. Is there a center that will hold? As the narrative moves ahead his hesitance, hiding, and forbearance will shift to signify a craving for interaction, reassurance, and definition. Do you have a sense of familiarity with this character as you shape him in response to your own experience and to

---

[17] See Eslinger, *Kingship* 405–407, for discussion of this careful equation.

these words? What do you recognize comfortably, perhaps compassionately, and what irritates you? What do you make of the storyteller, the narrating voice who has assembled this series of askings for us? In another longer work on King Saul I develop the notion that the players here, operating only dyadically, weave *in absentia* royal robes for the king to wear and only afterwards select the towering individual who is to don them.[18] Saul slips hesitantly into them, his discomfort palpable. The anomalies can be summarized best in a series of paradoxes that we have seen on the sketch pads and palettes of the "character artists" in "the narrator's studio." The tall man hiding. The restrainer of God's people holding his peace before their outrage. The asker compliant. The smallest as the tallest. The familiar shape with the new heart. The desire of all disdained by some. The failed seeker found. The ignominious feted. The king prophesying. The first son taken who will be a taker of sons. The *nagid* little aware. Though it may not yet be clear, this currently-reluctant monarch will cling ferociously to his throne. These paradoxes invite us to echo the question of the ne'er-do-wells: How can this save us?

---

[18] Barbara Green, *How Are the Mighty Fallen? A Dialogical Study of King Saul in 1 Samuel* (Sheffield: Sheffield Academic Press) forthcoming. As before, fuller discussion of a number of these points and others may be found in Polzin's ch. 3.

CHAPTER FOUR

Obedience Wanted, Wanting (1 Samuel 13–15)

> "At the very beginning . . . the narrator has set the stage by portraying a king deprived of information."
>
> Kenneth M. Craig,
> "Rhetorical Aspects of Questions"

Since Saul was so insistently requested it might seem that he should do well, have good support in his appointed role. Contrarily, we might suppose that given the conflicted manner of his asking there is little chance that the enterprise will prosper. How the king can walk well on his feet of clay is one way to frame the problem. But how he fails to do so is the story that will now unfold for our scrutiny and participation. Our particular charge is to calculate—make sense of and understand—why and how he fails and what significance his failure bears. It may seem easy enough, in the manner of television's first westerns, to put a light hat on a hero and a dark one on a villain, so that we can be reliably cued as to their virtue. But what should adorn the head of this king is not nearly so clear.

We are, however, given a more nuanced presentation. As this present chapter concludes I will offer a summary paragraph of what I think is fundamentally amiss. I will be building my case as we proceed here, referring you occasionally to scholars who hold different views. But part of your responsible reading, your answerability, is to work it out for yourself, however tentatively and provisionally. The lazy path is to decide Saul is wrong and thus with *carte blanche* find fault with every move he makes. You have perhaps been in situations where one person becomes so pervasively negative about another that nothing can ever be praised, everything is flawed. It is a reaction I hope we can avoid for Saul, and for God as well. Though Saul is our main focus, this is a biblical story and for many, Scripture. The representation of God's interaction in this long story is provocative for many, and we will take it up at the proper time.

The nub of what we will read is that Saul begins his reign "officially" at the start of chapter 13, is fired by the end of 15, and yet is still ruling by the end of chapter 31. His monarchy is short and long, its apparent end deferred past the moment of its actual demise. But how can Saul know how to be the first king? We can piece together his task from the places it was discussed in the last chapter: First, he is to rule over and fight for his people, put them on a par with other nations nearby (8:5-7, 19-20; 10:1). Second, and more specifically, he is both to save them from Philistines and also to "restrain" the people in some respect (9:15-17).[1] Third, he is charged to absorb and make workable the law of Deuteronomy (Deut 17:18-20), which foundationally specifies the relationship between YHWH and people (12:14-15, 20-25). The "what" is clearer than the "how." Additionally, we have not seen Saul receive even this meager information as clearly as it has been communicated to us. The first part of it came in conversations between Samuel and the elders, Samuel and God. The second portion was conferenced by deity to prophet. Though we can perhaps glimpse his tall self in the crowd Samuel addresses at Gilgal (ch. 12), the king is spoken *of* and not *to*. Even his third charge, the copy of the Law that the king is to have made for himself, seems handed past him by Samuel, to be stored up before God (10:25). We have not seen, will not see Saul collapsed at night, glasses awry, the lawbook fallen across his chest as he dozes off while perusing it. We may take heart from the presence of a prophet at his side, but Samuel will not be there for long. We remain, then, rooted in the genre of riddle, not quite so explicitly as in our first two chapters, but still at a remove from realism. This is not a historical sketch of an Early Iron Age king; it cannot give ready access to the failures of a historical Saul. It is the story of a monarch(y) whose asking is shown deficient from its roots.

There is another way to look at "Saul's asking," his failure of answerability. Polzin comments perceptively that "[Saul's] character zone is filled with doubt and uncertainty. Surrounded by a dubious aura, Saul is the epitome of a questionable choice . . . one who . . . continually asks questions."[2] Though I have maintained and will continue to promote my sense

---

[1] The last verb, typically translated as "rule," is actually "restrain." We will see several translation challenges in this part of the narrative.

[2] Robert M. Polzin, *Samuel and the Deuteronomist: A Literary Study of the Deuteronomic History: I Samuel* (San Francisco: Harper & Row, 1989) 103.

that the first king represents the whole experience of Israel with kings, what Polzin calls Israel's "disastrous romance with kingship,"[3] Saul is also a plausible human being. He is a self in a way that we, being selves too, can understand. Though each of us experiences ourself to be foundationally relational, in dialogue constantly with others at many levels—some so subtle that we are hardly aware of them—yet each of us, I hazard, feels a sort of weave at our center where things can catch, be braided, however loosely, into a pattern that feels, and often looks like "us," "me." Bakhtin's language for this phenomenon is to say that a human being (a hero in his language) must *posit* what is *given,* turn what comes toward us into something we have shaped with all we can bring to bear.[4] The answerable person takes what is given (some of the precepts, formulas, ritual, and principles, the situated details that comprise existence) and makes them workable in his or her own life. There is nothing of the cafeteria approach here; choices are made as carefully as possible, with great intentionality, since they accumulate and compose interactively the loose substance that makes an interrelating self. The raw material of our deeds and the shape we impose upon it—or the reality that takes shape as we act—must be seen for its interrelatedness.

The opposite, as we have seen in our introductory sweep through Bakhtin, is to alibi, to pretend. It is important to make a distinction here: we are not diagnosing character psychology directly, but listening in as discourse rages and reading ourselves. That is a fine distinction, so let me illustrate it from prosaic life. Let us suppose that on a given day an instructor of yours strides into the classroom, throws her books onto the desk, sweeps detritus of the last class into the wastebasket without retrieving the bits that fall to the floor, turns abruptly to erase the board, move the video viewer, roll up the screen, and so forth. The compressed energy behind all these moves is unusually rough, so the class falls silent, keeping one eye on her while also scanning peers. One student mouths to another, "She's mad because the faculty senate turned down her proposal yesterday," while another muses, "She's still upset about the basketball game last night." But a third says to himself, "Whatever the cause, I see the effect. Something tells

---

[3] Polzin, *Samuel and the Deuteronomist* 137–39. Robert Alter, *The David Story: A Translation with Commentary of 1 and 2 Samuel* (New York: W.W. Norton & Company, 1999) 83, makes a similar point: ". . . Saul's failed inquiry here participates in a larger pattern in his story: he is constantly seeking knowledge of what is about to happen . . . but this knowledge is repeatedly withheld from him."

[4] Mikhail Bakhtin, *Toward a Philosophy of the Act,* eds. Vadim Liapunov and Michael Holquist, trans. Vadim Liapunov (Austin: University of Texas Press, 1993) *passim,* but look at p. 42.

me to be ve-ee-rr-rry careful as I do my presentation today; how can I bring up the criticism of her article that I want to get onto the table so we can work with it?" We are closer here to the third than to the first two students. We will do our reading dialogically with the other, in this case Saul. But it is ourselves and our own assessing responses that we are able to speak for answerably. The portrait of the king—in positive and negative space— engages us to map ourselves, imaginatively.

This portion of our story is offered in two long scenes, chapters 13–14 featuring war with Philistines, chapter 15 war with Amalek. Each scene features some blend of interaction among king, prophet, and deity; the father-son motif is present, as is—oddly—the mother-son topos. Centrally posed is the managing of war and cult, which may strike us as an odd com- bination but would seem wholly unsurprising to the ancients. Though there is considerable other detail in each of the scenes, we will focus without skewing the narrative on what Saul does on three occasions (once in each chapter), how he is critiqued, how he takes rebuke. The issues of answer- ability will emerge as he talks with others, and as loudly when he falls silent. "What does Saul know and when does he know it" is a question that will absorb our energies. But we can ask the same about the prophet Samuel and the deity YHWH. *What* we are shown is failure: Saul's incapacity for answerability, both structurally and personally; *that* the monarch(y) fails is the central assertion. The *how* and *why*, though important, are secondary.

War with the Philistines: (1 Samuel 13–14)

In order to appreciate the "first firing" of the new king we must back up to the signs Samuel offered Saul to confirm the reliability of his anoint- ing (10:1-8). The prophet, having told Saul that when the signs came true he was to do "whatever your hand finds, for God is with you," simultane- ously attaches a rider: Go down to Gilgal, and await me seven days until I come to "make you know what you will do" [10:8, author's translation]. Saul registers no cavil over that odd blend at the time, and so we now all approach it again. This present Philistine engagement, like that of chapter 2, looms suddenly and goes badly (13:1-7). Jonathan, a young man we also meet unexpectedly, strikes a blow that riles masses of Philistines: as many as the sand at the seashore, the narrator observes. Though scholars find it odd, Saul seems to pause in the midst of the danger and gather his troops at Gilgal to offer sacrifices.[5] The narrator assists Saul's cause here by noting

---

[5] Scholars are resourceful here, of course. The fact that there has already been a Gilgal scene where Samuel made a lot of information known may suggest that the fourth of the

circumstances. Saul's troops have already disappeared into caves, holes, crags, tombs, wells, and even across the Jordan. He is understandably already beleaguered by a foe as numerous as sand on the seashore, but he waits his seven days. When his people continue to slip away for one reason or another, Saul calls for the sacrifices and offers them himself (13:8-9). As he is finishing, Samuel appears and questions him about this deed (v. 11).

Though Christian readers are predisposed to fault a king for doing a priestly task, that point rises neither here nor elsewhere in these early stories, where the king typically presides on cultic occasions. Scholars have a propensity to cite Saul for obsession with ritual, which I think is similarly misplaced.[6] So we must listen to the king and prophet converse. First Saul: "When I saw that the people were slipping away from me, and that you did not come within the days appointed, and that the Philistines were mustering at Michmash, I said, 'Now the Philistines will come down upon me at Gilgal, and I have not entreated the favor of the LORD'; so I forced myself and offered the burnt offering" (13:11-12). Samuel is shortly to characterize this move very negatively, but before he does so, what do *we* hear? First, Saul and the narrator agree, largely, their speech intersecting comfortably to reinforce each other, which helps Saul's case. But Saul's talk about the others and his own self-quotation clamor for attention. His words bear a subtle but clear tendency to blame Samuel, the Philistines, the people, even the deity: too many Philistines, too few Israelites, a worship urgency, and absent prophet. And so, says the king (long-windedly in twenty-seven Hebrew words),[7] I forced/restrained myself to do it. His

---

signs from ch. 10 already occurred. But there is an obvious effort here to make this present scene of 13:8-15 connect to the prophet's words of 10:7-8, and with that we must cope, clumsy though the splicing may now look to us.

   [6] See Polzin, *Samuel and the Deuteronomist* 130–37, for leads on Saul's obsession with ritual. The act of doing such a liturgy before a battle seems unmotivated in this passage (see Ralph W. Klein, *1 Samuel* [Waco: Word Books, 1983] 127); nor is it clear simply from this context exactly what the offerings are for: to stem desertions (so Jan P. Fokkelman, *Narrative Art and Poetry in the Books of Samuel: Volume II: The Crossing Fates* [Assen, The Netherlands: Van Gorcum, 1986] 38), or to sacrifice instead of fight (Peter D. Miscall, *1 Samuel: A Literary Reading* [Bloomington: Indiana University Press, 1986] 87). The significance may lie in the fact that the same elements cluster in the next battle (1 Samuel 15). David Gunn, *The Fate of King Saul: An Interpretation of a Biblical Story* (Sheffield: JSOT Press, 1980) 34, rather lonely in the field, speculates that Saul has not broken any general command of which we know, and if he violated a specific one it was ambiguous in its phrasing (p. 39). Gunn concludes that the reason for the rejection remains unclear (p. 67).

   [7] Miscall, *1 Samuel* 85. Scholars struggle with the exact nuance of the verb here, with some preferring the sense of the king forcing himself against some barrier and others liking the sense of restraining himself from something tempting, such as fleeing. See Polzin, *Samuel and the Deuteronomist* 129, for the discussion.

words pointing out the flaws of the others bring in their wake testimony of
his own inability to restrain them. Additionally, Saul seems to find it a
struggle to manage his own role, and when he pulls himself together he
somehow errs.[8] His language about his own process (the word translated
"forced myself") itself implies that he had to place some effort between
what he did and some alternative behavior. His worship project seems out
of place in terms of God's character, since God has demanded nothing of
the sort in any scene that we have witnessed. Saul shows himself unable—
not necessarily unwilling—to perform the charge he has been given to lead
the people successfully against Philistines. Finally, the narrator edge can
be seen to turn slightly against the king, since we were shown Saul doing
the deed with no inner process expressed; when he brings it forth *ex post
facto* it seems lame. The narrator had other choices here.

Samuel rejoins at once, appraising, evaluating: "You have done foolishly; you have not kept the commandment of the LORD, which he commanded you. The LORD would have established your kingdom over Israel
forever, but now your kingdom will not continue; the LORD has sought a
man after his own heart; and the LORD has appointed him to be ruler . . .
because you have not kept what the LORD commanded you" (13:13-14).
Harsh and final. What can we notice here? What command? we may first
ask. If we recall Samuel's "fourth sign" (10:18), then it seems clear that
Saul was to await his prophet. At 9:16-17 he was urged to rescue people
from Philistines and to restrain them; at 12:14-15 king and people are en-
joined to obey God. So it is not utterly clear how he is to proceed. But
whatever directions Samuel has in mind, he calls Saul's action a foolish
and radical disobedience of a command of God. Is there more here than
poor timing on Saul's part, or on Samuel's for that matter? We need to note
that it is only Samuel's word we heard calling for sacrifices at Gilgal, and
in fact only the prophet's report of God's feeling about the dynastic firing.
Prophets, no less than others, deal in fragile, frangible words. My point is
not so much that Samuel did not hear God's discourse as that he does not
communicate it directly or unambiguously to Saul. The command we heard
is Samuel's; the promise just withdrawn we have not heard proffered. We
have heard such eternal promises revoked before, when the nameless man
of God fires the Elides (1 Samuel 2:27-36). Though Samuel does not comment directly on Saul's need to appease God before a battle or link the urge
to placate with vanishing troops, the words he does speak allow the con-

---

[8] J. Cheryl Exum, *Tragedy and Biblical Narrative: Arrows of the Almighty* (Sheffield:
Sheffield Academic Press, 1992) 162 n. 56, develops the same information in a rather different way.

struction that the king did what was not wanted and failed to do what had been explicitly asked. The likelihood of this explanation increases, since it will be made explicit in the next military/cultic episodes. The point is not that Saul misread the manual, made a dumb mistake. However trivial the pretext may look to us, the prophet characterizes it as a radical failure of the fundamental charge of obedience.[9] On a cultic/military occasion Saul cannot lead well. He has dismissed and regathered his men; the battle commences not at Saul's command but when Jonathan strikes. Saul is delayed by his absent prophet. The king sees his troops are going and the enemy is massing; alone and without recourse to advice he acts precipitously, to appease God. The scene culminates in a rejection of sons. Saul's heirs are fired for a fault of their father. Or, if we turn back to the start of the episode, we might construe that the whole situation blows up because Jonathan, who we shortly learn is none other than Saul's son and presumed heir, goes offsides in the initial play of this battle (13:3).[10] Can sons save their fathers? Or do dynastic sons bring down their ancestral enterprises? Saul, we must note, makes no reply to Samuel, who departs as Saul turns back to the battle. The firing is more significant than the particulars of the cause, but what can we say to explain the deed?

And it is indeed father-son interaction that absorbs the next portion of this long event (13:15–14:23). Certain commentators make an excellent case for this son being a foil for the father,[11] but it is not quite simply that Jonathan does better and Saul worse. As the Philistine battle continues Saul rallies his troops, few as they have become, keeping them together as the Philistines split and move out across the landscape. But the precipitating move, as before, is Jonathan's. He provokes the opponent once again, gauging the reaction of the Philistines to the moves of himself and his single companion as signifying the cooperation of God.[12] The team of Jonathan, his armor-bearer, and the deity kills some twenty of the enemy

---

[9] Some scholars (e.g., Alter, *David Story* 72, and Gunn, *Fate* 66) sense entrapment here, which is a possibility. But if we stipulate that we are not watching an actual scene but reading a puzzle that must represent a complex situation in a series of (for us) three points, then things shift. To read some diverse views, consult David Jobling, *1 Samuel* (Collegeville: The Liturgical Press, 1998) 85–86, and especially Exum, *Tragedy.*

[10] For detail on this possibility see Diana V. Edelman, *King Saul in the Historiography of Judah* (Sheffield: Sheffield Academic Press, 1991) 77.

[11] Edelman, *Saul* 83; Fokkelman, *Fates* 61; Jobling, *1 Samuel* 94–95.

[12] Jonathan's small rituals that seem successful and approved at the surface of the story caution us about making too many confident calls about Saul's obsessive piety. What I would point out is that at least in these scenes of chs.13 and 14 Jonathan's plans work out more felicitously than do Saul's, show better coordination with the realm of the rather hidden God.

and catches the attention of Saul, who musters, counts, and learns who is at the heart of the skirmish. Though the king, assisted by Ahijah, great-grandson of Eli, begins a consultation with ark or ephod,[13] Saul breaks it off and engages the Philistines, with one result being the return of many who had earlier slithered away. Saul's six hundred swell to some ten thousand, and battle is engaged and the Philistines routed, a deed the narrator characterizes as YHWH's saving. And so we come to a second military-cultic move of the king (14:24-48). First we will examine the "what" and then the "why."

The narrator, in some apparent sympathy with Saul's situation at Gilgal, has no such presumption here. "Now Saul committed a very rash act on that day . . ." the narrator evaluates for us before we hear what it is. Saul, we learn, enjoins by oath that none shall take food "until I have been avenged on my enemies" (14:24), language that grates against the more collegial language of chapters 8–12 and the narrator's attribution of victory to YHWH. Two things go wrong. First, Jonathan, who either does not hear (we recall he has gone off on his own) or does not heed (the Hebrew allows for that possibility as well), tastes honey when the company spy a dripping honeycomb. He is the only one to do so, and no one tells him of the oath against taking food until Jonathan has violated it. The king's son appears unperturbed and, perhaps rather uncharacteristically from a number of vantage points, airs his view that the command was "troublous"[14] and ill-advised (14:25-30).[15] Second, the troops who seem to have coped well enough with the Philistines, now hungry, the narrator informs us, swoop prematurely on spoils and slaughter livestock to end their fast without properly draining the blood. Saul blurts an odd accusation that the people have played him false, but hastily erects a stone where "kosher" slaughter can be done—his first altar, the narrator comments rather ominously. But when, wanting to push ahead afterwards to mop up the Philistine slaughter, he inquires *(sh'l)*, as is his character to do, God goes silent—more silent, we might be tempted to say (14:31-37).

---

[13] Since the ark is under sedation at Kiriath-jearim it seems unlikely that it would appear on site here, though that is what the text says.

[14] Alter, *David Story* 81, traces the verb "troubled" of 14:21 to the action of stirring up mud from the bottom of a pond and refers us to its use in Judg 11:35, which directs us to another story where a father's oath endangers a child.

[15] Views include: the oath is too imprecisely worded (Edelman, *Saul* 88); the king careens from deficit to surplus of religion (Fokkelman, *Fates* 62); piety leads to trouble (Gunn, *Fate* 68–69); "fatal impetuosity" (P. Kyle McCarter, *1 Samuel. A New Translation with Introduction and Commentary* [Garden City, N.Y.: Doubleday, 1980] 240); dumb oath, excessive vengeance, poor timing (Miscall, *1 Samuel* 93–94).

With no prophet on site, Saul holds a sort of trial to ascertain the reason for what he has interpreted as divine displeasure, assuming automatically and quickly that someone has sinned (14:38-46). Reinforcing his speech with another oath, he pledges, ". . . even if it is my son Jonathan, he shall surely die." With at first no response from people as well as deity, Saul starts the casting of lots.[16] As before, the casting process moves expeditiously, requiring only two steps (the Saul family on one side, the ten thousand on the other); the Saulides are indicated at once, which we must notice is a bit unexpected, given the episode of improper slaughter. When father and son are counterpoised, Jonathan is taken. When questioned, he readily admits that he violated the oath of his father and expresses his readiness to die. His earlier second-guessing is conspicuously absent. That is, he does not say, "I violated (though inadvertently) the oath you solemnly (though foolishly) laid upon the people as we were finishing up this remarkable deliverance from God, a taste of honey, for which I am about to die." So though Jonathan seems noteworthy for his refusal to alibi (contrasted with his father who is becoming prone to it), he also stands out here—though not at the start of the chapter—for avoiding religious categories when they might have been used. Saul agrees with Jonathan quickly, eagerly, again indicting his inability to restrain his own son. It is only the people, also unrestrained by king or lots, who insist that Jonathan shall not die for the work of God he has accomplished (14:37-46). The narrator refuses us access to any other discourse and detail. Saul, rebuked, makes no reply and the narrator breaks off the story, simply noting that the battle ceased, each side retreating to its territory.

Once again, the chapter concludes with a wider view of Saul's reign, almost as though it were over: successful battles (14:47-48, 52), including with Philistines. And, the narrator relates, Saul has three sons (named), two daughters (named), a wife (named), a commander-in-chief (named as kin), and we are reminded of Saul's lineage. But the firstborn son Jonathan stands under death sentence, result of both his father's foolishness and his own deed, reprieved with ambiguous wisdom. God's view of these matters is available indirectly at best. Is God pleased with these things? The story slides us along to conclude so unless we recall the firing of the priestly house of Elides and Saul's season of losses so far in communicating with God. But once again I think the issue for us is not whether Jonathan shall die or not, die justly or otherwise. That the king is fallen and his line under

---

[16] Kenneth M. Craig, Jr., "Rhetorical Aspects of Questions Answered with Silence in 1 Samuel 14:37 and 28:6," *CBQ* 56 (1994) 222–23, points out a threefold repetition of Saul's reaching out to blame the other: in ch. 13, here in 14, and we know also coming up in 15.

sentence of non-existence is the "what" of this episode, as in the one previous. The how and why root in Saul's mistimed askings and his flimsy answerings.

War with the Amalekites (1 Samuel 15)

The third major event portrayed as context for Saul's firing replays the coordinates of the first two in sufficient detail to suggest that we are to see it as a third point enabling us to draw a straight line in our search to locate Saul's incapacity for answerability. The episode is well studied in scholarship and turns on some thorny problems in wider biblical studies, notably the topics of sacral war and ban (military execution of certain foes).[17] There is not space to review all the relevant factors or texts, but in short, there is no easy case to be made against Saul here from the general law of *herem* or ban. In fact, the general law, its implementation in other passages, and even the specifics of this situation lead me to the conclusion that to indict Saul for a technical breach of timing or to cite him for a trivial infraction is to miss the point. Once again, a serious violation of a fundamental responsibility is enacted here, a "what" that precedes our looking for the "why and how." There is something more serious at stake here than a careless royal slip-up, a confusing and angry intermediary, or a capricious deity. We will, as before, break out first the deed itself (directions in vv. 1-3 and enactment in 4-9) and then six rounds of discussion (vv. 10-31) that pick up more conclusively the question of "what next," how to "go back" after this event.

The directions, buttressed by prophetic authority and then in phraseology of divine speech (from men to women, adult to infant, large to small domesticated animal) are: slay all. But though the directions, presented in God's direct discourse to be communicated to Saul by Samuel, are clear in their general outline (spare none), they are not consistent in their address (addressing a mix of singular and plural persons, the exact issue that will become disputed) or, in the event, sufficiently specific as to timing (when Saul's deed is complete). But their nuance is really not the point that is under development; it is difficult to give foolproof directions. What we

---

[17] For a fresh set of suggestions regarding ban as well as a brief discussion of older scholarship consult Richard D. Nelson, *Joshua: A Commentary* (Louisville: Westminster John Knox, 1997) 17–20, 89–90, 93–106, 111–13, in particular. The Deuteronomy legislation (13:12 and 20:10-17) stipulates that the ban is to be exercised upon local people, and upon occasion spoil can evidently be taken, though not always, as we see from Joshua 6–8. Nelson stresses that despite superficial similarity the realms of sacrifice and dedication-to-destruction or ban are not to be mixed.

also learn is that an ancient score from the time of the Exodus is to be settled. Saul is here given a special task, one rooted in the primordial relationship between YHWH and the people brought forth from Egypt, addressed at Horeb, and given a new land. That he fails to do it satisfactorily differs in detail from his prior failures with Philistines but reinforces those lapses strongly.

The narrator's description of the enactment seems equally comprehensive. Saul smites Amalek, the narrator characterizes, from Havilah to Shur (near Egypt). He seizes Agag king of Amalek alive but kills all the rest of the people with the sword. And, reiterates the narrator with both ambiguity and clarity, "Saul and the people spared Agag, and the best of the sheep and of the cattle and of the fatlings, and the lambs, and all that was valuable, and would not utterly destroy them; but all that was despised and worthless they utterly destroyed" (15:9). One person and some animals spared; the main person and the best animals saved, with the inferior ones slain. The erosion of Saul's case begins before he speaks. It is not utterly clear exactly who did what—king or people—but in any case we know already that the fate of king and people is inseparable (12:25). Before we listen to the ensuing conversation between king and prophet we have a general sense of what happened, though it needs refining. If, as I have stipulated, the issue here needs to be important and not simply technical, then Saul has to have a chance. Can Saul's choice regarding Agag be an answerable deed, like Joshua's decision to let Rahab and her family go, though that choice was contrary to explicit directions (Joshua 2)? Though he is going to be adjudged wrong, I need to slow us from thinking it utterly obvious.

But again from the narrator a bit of preliminary information weighs in crucially. Without much of a narrative join, the word of YHWH comes to Samuel in direct discourse: "'I regret/repent that I made Saul king, for he has turned back from me and my words he does not hold up'" [15:11, author's translation]. It is vital to note that only we and Samuel hear this utterance; it is not passed on to Saul. Additionally, the divine feeling of regret/repentance is all we hear, at most God's announcement of a deed, though Samuel will move the words into policy before the end of the passage. Though we next learn that Samuel is angry at something and cries out to YHWH all that night, there is no response from God to prophet that is shared with us. There is a vast discrepancy of information as Samuel proceeds, in our presence, toward Saul, a handicap under which Saul also labored in the preceding episode. And we hear that while prophet and deity are dealing with one set of problems about his deed Saul is erecting a monument. The news, which we may think implies Saul's clear conscience, in fact only makes it clear that his judgment continues bad.

As the two men engage each other in conversation we listen to a fundamentally uneven exchange. In *round one* (15:14-15) Samuel disputes Saul's claim of having done as he was instructed, the noise of lowing animals in the prophet's ears serving as evidence that some have escaped the ban. Saul blames the people. In *round two* (v. 16) Samuel hushes Saul's alibi and states his intention to make known *(hgd)* God's views, to which Saul replies: speak. *Round three* (vv. 17-21) brings us closer to the heart of the matter. Drawing on Saul's former description of himself as "small" (9:21), Samuel reminds him he is head and king, commanded to do a task, the directions for which Samuel also brings forward again, but skillfully replaces the command "to strike" with the verb "complete," thus underlining a clear defect on the king's part.[18] Samuel's next words take question form, loaded questions (and answers) with tendentious phraseology: "'Why did you not obey the voice of the LORD? Why did you swoop down on the spoil and do what was evil in the sight of the LORD?'" As before, the prophet charges a failure to heed the voice of YHWH: Samuel claims that Saul replaced that obedience with evil (repeating now the substance though not the words of YHWH the prophet heard in the night [15:10, 19]). What we do not hear Samuel say aloud to Saul is God's "I repent/regret making Saul king."[19] Saul's response reiterates what he *did* accomplish, how he *did* comply, but once again he points to the actions of the people as flawed in their desire to stockpile sacrificial offerings for Gilgal; he not only blames them but also redirects our attention to Gilgal, site of his earlier incapacity to restrain the people. As twice before, he points at others while signaling his own flaw.

Samuel's next words (*round four*, 15:22-25), attending first to Saul's mention of sacrifices, maintain that obedience is more important than sacrifice (without denying the possibility that one can do both). He then labels Saul's deed of non-hearing as divination, rebellion, stubbornness, idolatry. The conclusion of this unit for Samuel is rejection, the word we met in 8:7, what I have preferred to call firing. Samuel clarifies, emphasizes: because you "fired" God's word, God fires you from being king. The prophet, we need to observe, is the one who has moved the deity's words from an expression of feeling to an action step, unprompted in any way we can witness. Saul concedes: "I have sinned." But his next words seem fatal

---

[18] We have another instance where a translator makes a choice for smoother English by perhaps eliminating a nuance preserved in Hebrew and helpful for the story.

[19] Miscall's way of saying it is that Samuel's words seem to exceed YHWH's (*Samuel* 101–108). See Fokkelman, *Fates* 97, for a chart setting forth the elements of these matters comparatively.

to me, since his acknowledgment slides immediately into blame of the people. Saul's alibi underlines that he violated his monarchic charge as fundamentally as possible, by obeying people instead of God, by caving in to rather than restraining the people. Then he urges Samuel to accompany him to do sacrifices. In *round five* (vv. 26-27) Samuel (harder on the penitent than God most typically is) verbally refuses Saul's invitation to turn toward God with him and reiterates his rejection/firing language, although (or perhaps because) Saul has not alluded to this part of Samuel's speech. Saul seems to have missed the larger issue of his royal repudiation and to be caught on the question of immediate appearances. Saul's only response is a gesture—grasping "his" robe (someone grasps someone's robe—ambiguous in the Hebrew).

So in the last *round* (*six:* vv. 28-31) Samuel interprets the gesture, linking it to a point he now makes for the third time: "'The LORD has torn the kingdom of Israel from you this very day and has given it to a neighbor of yours, who is better than you are.'" This word—good, better—matches what we heard from Samuel in 13:13, though we must again take care to note that we have not heard it credited in direct discourse to YHWH. YHWH has regretted the choice of Saul (15:11), but that is not the same as removing him. And Samuel here in fact contravenes what we heard him hear from God: the glory of Israel does not change his mind like a mortal.[20] Hence the prophet has laid bare the core of the situation: the hearts of deity and king are not well-aligned and are relentlessly moving toward cross-purposes. Samuel does not speak of God with utter verifiability here, perhaps undermining our confidence in him elsewhere; or more precisely, the slight slippages may slow us from assuming utter transparency between God and prophet, as with prophet and king, king and people, and so forth. Language rarely remains utterly exact and equivalent as it passes from mouth to mouth, person to person. Saul's rejoinder to that word is to repeat his plea of round five: "'I have sinned; yet honor me now before the elders of my people and before Israel, and return with me so I may worship the LORD your God.'" Saul's hope for honor from Samuel is perhaps too reminiscent of Eli and sons (2:30, 4:18); in any case the narrator concludes that Samuel acceded, turned back with him.[21] It may be as well that honor (and its Hebrew link to "heavy") has become an ironic word since the dynast Eli topples from it to his death (4:18); in such a reading the prophet concurs

---

[20] Alter, *David Story* 92, suggests that the prophet says God will not change his mind about changing his mind.

[21] Everett Fox, *Give Us a King! Samuel, Saul and David* (New York: Schocken, 1999) 73.

with Saul's wish to fall, enacts it prophetically and cultically while Saul, prone, entreats God.

The story seems concluded, except for the fate of the Amalekite king (vv. 32-35), who stands under condemnation, whose life has been claimed though not yet ended. In one of the storyteller's vivid moments that seem to reprise the story of kings in one brilliant point, the already condemned king steps forward, little aware of what has transpired, assuming perhaps that the time of danger is passed for him. He is shown wrong in an instant, as Samuel, speaking words of maternal bereavement, cuts him down. The king is dead, scarcely recognizing his own precariousness. The narrator notes that prophet and king (Saul) do not meet again, an inauspicious note for a king who needs all the help he can get. Samuel, we are told, grieves for Saul (in what particular we do not know) and YHWH repents of having made him king.

Conclusions

We have seen two aspects of failure in three orchestrations. First, *that* Saul has failed as monarch is shown in his inability to do his job. His war with the Philistines bogs down after the debacle with Jonathan and the broken oaths; the Philistines will return eventually to bring Saul down. The Amalekites, against logic, also elude him (since they recur elsewhere in this story and in other biblical narrative); one of them as well will make himself prominent as Saul dies. Saul hears poorly in his job: he has no reliable access to God, an incapacity to understand and obey his prophet, a tendency to heed the people. He cannot restrain them, his son, himself. And globally Saul refuses to listen to the evidence of all these things. Second, the explication—the *how* and *why*—of Saul's inanswerability as a human being is also made clear. Saul's character shows no coherent self. He asks, as is his Hebrew name identity, failing in each case to mesh with his interlocutors; his projects go off balance as he fails to collaborate. Having omitted his responsibility of ruminating on *Torah,* he has nothing wise to bring forth when occasion demands it. His alibis, which fill his speech, blame others and shift onus from himself but ultimately boomerang, since they testify all too clearly to his unraveling edges. Bakhtin's notion of pretender fits Saul well: lacking a coherent center, he relies instead on ritual and role, careening from excess to defect, from malleability to rigidity, from frenzy to inaction. His gestures may not be insincere, but since they are not truthful in a fuller sense they collapse ultimately as sham. Both as monarch and as man, Saul is shown utterly incapable of promoting the relatedness between God and people, the "one thing needful," not least because he himself evidences no relationship with God, little with any character we have seen, and minimal self-knowledge. God seems to back away from Saul, not so much contend with as withdraw from him. The given for our storyteller is *that* kingship fails; to account for it is our readers' challenge. I have told you how and why I think Saul most foundationally fails. What do you think?

CHAPTER FIVE

Suspecting the Dreaded (1 Samuel 16–19)

"[W]hat was previously a gift now becomes a torment."

Everett Fox, *Give Us a King!*

Having set up Saul to show us the inadequacy of the monarchy and the weakness of the monarch, I will now explore the texture of those claims. We will listen as Saul talks, making himself most known when he least senses anyone attending. Think, for a moment, about the phenomenon of selftalk, the inner tape that presumably we all play in our own heads— I say presumably because each of us hears only our own and can at best assume that other people do the same. What do you talk about to yourself, and how do you set up the conversations? Is your selftalk often defensive, justifying yourself in circumstances where you feel blamed? Or is it triumphant, featuring a clever you vanquishing frustrated opponents? For whom is your selftalk shaped, besides yourself? It is my experience that we can learn a lot by listening in on ourselves, and of course by adding tapes to our repertoire, for example the Psalms. But that is another topic. With some fresh thoughts on our own selftalk we will listen to Saul's general discourse and especially to his private ruminations.

This section is delimited by David's sojourn at court: As we begin here, the spirit-of-YHWH moves from Saul to David (16:1-13) and Saul invites David to his court (16:14-23); by the end YHWH's spirit opposes Saul (who is opposing David) and David flees the court (19:18-24). Between these two edges we will listen in on four episodes involving Saul and his children, now intensively involved with David (17:1-54; 17:55–18:16;

18:17-30; 19:1-17). Once David is on the scene it is difficult not to make him the center of attention; indeed, that is part of the problem in the story: everyone's focus on David! We will stick by Saul, who will lead us into the snarl of the rest of the characters in any case.

Our charge here is to see if by scrutinizing discourse we can get a sense of what Saul lacks, what he desires, and how and why it eludes him. A good deal of this chapter will involve his interaction with his own children and with the young David, whom Saul invites, by degrees, into the royal family circle. But we will also hear Saul struggle in relation to God's spirit, which seems to let him down badly. Without losing the institutional and social piece of the riddle Saul is showing us, we will concentrate here on the human and personal side of the character, his "strugglous" language. And while discussing Saul I will also suggest more explicitly how a character like Saul helps us if we read him deeply and attend to what we are doing when we read.

Saul loses Y_HWH's spirit to David (16:1-13)

In this short section where Saul seems absent we have a phenomenon Bakhtin calls hybridized speech. To explain it quickly: The narrator and characters pick up and reuse each other's speech from some earlier occasion(s), which has an effect (among others) of helping us make links we might otherwise miss. If you compare carefully you will see to what extent the language used for the selection of David replays what we saw for Saul: divine choice revealed to the prophet at the key moment, the young man chosen from "following animals," brought to a sacrifice that was ready but delayed, the chosen one rushed by God's spirit.[1] More important, we hear God in direct discourse own up to what we had heard previously only from Samuel: God has fired Saul from being king (16:1), a chain reaching back to the firing of God by the people (15:23, 26; 10:19; 8:7-8); what is restated here is the toggling, mutual disintegration of the relationship between deity and people that the king had been assigned to guard. Unlike Samuel, God never says that the firing of Saul has come about *because* Israel fired God; Saul's firing, as we have already had occasion to see and will continue to watch, comes about because of his incapacity to mind the relationship of Y_HWH and Israel. Saul cannot do that job, and so he must make way for someone who can. If we have harbored the notion that God, who selected

---

[1] Jan P. Fokkelman, *Narrative Art and Poetry in the Books of Samuel: Volume II: The Crossing Fates* (Assen, The Netherlands: Van Gorcum, 1986) 112–26.

Saul, will stand by him, it must now go. Saul is not personally rejected, but he is terminated from his position because he failed to fill it well.

Saul is also, again, shown "terminated" in another sense. Samuel is grieving over him, God points out (16:1). Samuel will also cut Saul dead in the sense of not speaking to him again until the fateful scene in chapter 28 where Saul has his old prophet raised from the dead, only to hear Samuel tell him he is about to join him in the world below. So though Saul has more time aboveground and more adventures to go, he is a walking dead man. Already his obituary has been printed (14:47-51). His offspring have been pronounced redundant (13:13-14) and the heir apparent sentenced to death: Jonathan lives under a speech act of capital punishment, the sentence commuted but not canceled. And, strangely, Saul begins now also to be shown to be dead-*ly*. Though heretofore he has seemed mostly mild and pliable, even insecure and manipulable—not least by Samuel—now the prophet fears him (16:2) and others will soon learn to do so. When Samuel registers his fear of Saul to God, God does not contest it, though he overrides it.

As several scholars have pointed out, the motif word binding this section is "seeing," which you can pick up even in English.[2] How do Bethlehem's elders see Samuel as the prophet approaches their village? How does Samuel look at, appraise, and miss-see the qualities of Jesse's seven sons? How can a father fail to see, overlook his last son? Who spies nervous Samuel going to Bethlehem, and who is attentive when David is anointed king? The inscrutable watching of God is perhaps the heart of this scene, this seeing: how does God choose David, why did God choose Saul? What do we know about how God sees any of us? In a few short verses all these topics are on the table for our scrutiny, and for the most part they are open questions, not much foreclosed by being made known. The clearest voice is, perhaps, YHWH's, which gives us mostly negative information: Don't assume we see the same, God says to the seer! I look deeper in, you more at the surface (16:7).[3]

---

[2] A number of scholars identify the importance of the word *r'h*/see in this unit (and earlier): Robert Alter, *The David Story: A Translation with Commentary of 1 and 2 Samuel* (New York: W. W. Norton, 1999) 95; Diana V. Edelman, *King Saul in the Historiography of Judah* (Sheffield: Sheffield Academic Press, 1991) 112 (who also alerts us to concomitant blindness); Fokkelman, *Fates* 114; Peter D. Miscall, *1 Samuel: A Literary Reading* (Bloomington: Indiana University Press, 1986) 118; Robert M. Polzin, *Samuel and the Deuteronomist: A Literary Study of the Deuteronomic History: 1 Samuel* (San Francisco: Harper & Row, 1989) 152. Polzin reminds us to ask who sees and how deeply, reviewing for us how much insight has lacked so far (p. 153).

[3] Polzin, *Samuel and the Deuteronomist* 154, observes that in this story all human seeing is deficient (13:14; 15:29; 16:7).

The last point I would offer here involves the "switching of the spirit," which leaves Saul for David (16:13-14). It is easy for Christians to conflate this Hebrew Bible spirit of God with the trinitarian Holy Spirit and hence read Saul's case as really dire. I think it is not a helpful move to make. The topic is vast. But I urge the working hypothesis that in this story the breath or wind-of-God (hence the translation of "spirit") is God's shared agency for rule over Israel. The judges occasionally were lent it (e.g., Samson) and it lodged with Saul perhaps more long-term. But once Saul has been fired, it goes from him.[4] And—crucial point—once Saul resists his firing, digs in and refuses to vacate the post he is placing himself in opposition to God's choices and at heavy cost. God does not so much "reject" Saul as Saul sets his own sense of himself-as-king over against God and will spend his energy resisting. You may think that Saul has done no such thing yet, but I think the contretemps between Saul and Samuel in 15:24-31 offers a view of Saul refusing to take his "pink slip" out of the envelope but rather pushing it underneath an old pile of junk mail.

Saul (first) invites David to court (16:14-23)

Seeing remains central, binding the parts of the story closely together. We are back to some direct watching of Saul and notice what his servants see, and what they say (skipping momentarily the narrator remark of 16:14). The king's servants watch him tormented by an evil spirit they link to God, and they address that diagnosis to Saul directly. Desiring to help, they suggest a musician to soothe Saul when he is tormented. It is an interesting prescription on which we cannot linger, except to remark that they seem unscandalized by what they see, unafraid of Saul, and confident of their antidote. The narrator's voice slides in with their words, confirming—or doubling—the root cause of the problem: Saul's relationality with God. It is my own sense of knowing Saul's struggle to retain the throne despite God's contrary wishes that helps me specify the spirit as I do: not something God has devised to ruin Saul but something that complicates their common territory, which is rulership over Israel.

Next Saul, like God, the vast discrepancy in viewpoint notwithstanding, selects David for the royal court.[5] Saul, not alluding to what the servants have said about his condition—another refusal to acknowledge the firing—joins his assent to their words: Yes, get me such a one. They have

---

[4] Everett Fox, *Give Us A King! Samuel, Saul and David* (New York: Schocken, 1999) 81, reminds us that thus spirit is not a separate entity but some kind of supplement.

[5] Polzin, *Samuel and the Deuteronomist* 152.

urged him to seek—not the verb of asking that names and characterizes Saul, but a near synonym—and he agrees. A single voice speaks up to describe a candidate, detailing for us the qualities of a king, catching some of the language used of Saul's choosing in chapters 9–10. Most freighted is the word "good," which is used multiple times in this four-chapter section for David, reminding us—if not Saul—of Samuel's words of 15:28, where he indicates that God has already "seen to" a better (a good-er) man than Saul to be king. Get (literally "see to it for me") a good man, says Saul, inhabiting, but ironically, the previous speech of deity and prophet.[6] As we well know, the appraisal of what is good and what not is often painfully a matter of viewing angle. And so it will be for Saul. Saul bids his replacement come near, abstractly at v. 17 and then specifically: "Send me your son David who is with the sheep," the king requests (16:19). David enters Saul's court as musician-healer and also as armor-bearer.

Saul's blind choosing here will become characteristic of him as the story develops. His poor eyesight, limited insight, is at one level not his fault. Of course he does not—cannot—know that David is already the selected anointed of God, but my construction of Saul shows him steadfastly refusing any information on that topic because he so dreads to hear it. Saul here dreads something and does not suspect it, even as he bids it come close. Soon he will be more alert to its nearness and, fearing his own removal, assists it to happen. It is a place where Saul shows me a moment into which I can imaginatively step—not pretending to be a king but feeling akin to a rather morally myopic human who tends to push away self-knowledge lest it be worse than he wants to know. It is the dynamic I recognize, the refusal to know what is patent to those around me, and I can see *when Saul does it* the futility, indeed the counterproductivity of the gesture. It is a poignant moment when the old king welcomes the new one. Rather than see Saul as ridiculous in it, I see the moment as contributing helpfully to the quest for self-knowledge that transformative reading relies upon. But in any case the narrator's summative comment is that "David came to Saul and entered Saul's service. Saul loved him greatly, and he became his armor-bearer" (16:21). Everyone loves David when he arrives in court; that will be the ostensible problem. And indeed David's harp-playing soothes Saul, loosens him up, broadens his self, the narrator says, using a Hebrew word cognate with the word for spirit.[7]

---

[6] Edelman, *Saul* 118. In fact, she points out that Saul's command to others "to espy" a good/skilled man has peculiar resonance with God's description of his own action in regard to Jesse's sons (16:1, 6-7).

[7] Alter, *David Story* 100, comments that the verbal root shared by "spirit" and "relief" implies breadth or space that removes constraint.

Saul (first) invites David to be king (17:1-54)

We have next a long and probably familiar story of the Philistine giant Goliath. The stress on seeing continues here; the chapter is presented very visually.[8] Since we are sticking resolutely to Saul here—which does not preclude your looking at many other things, simply my writing about them—we will keep the "old king" in our sights. First, as we meet Goliath (17:1-11) we are presented with a tall leader who is apparently so covered with armor that he seems invincible; but such is not the case, as all are about to learn. His vulnerability is hidden for the moment, although biblical scholars claim to deduce it as the giant's armor is verbally surveyed.[9] His speech is bombastic, pompous, denigrating, and ultimately self-defeating since his words attract, almost invite the attention and response of his nemesis. Have we seen such a tall character before? In case we are uncertain, we are told that the giant has an armor-bearer to carry the great shield before him (17:7). The king's self sheltered behind "the gear" can, if we make the verbal link, cast us back to Saul's ducking amid the gear as the lots of his selecting are falling out in his favor. Goliath is, at the discourse level, a stand-in for Saul.

The opponent the giant is about to face is his foil in a number of ways. As the young David is redescribed for us as though we have not met him,[10] we follow him from Bethlehem to Saul's camp, watch him enter and stash his supplies with the quartermaster and join the demoralized Israelite fighters (17:12-30). As Goliath's words reverberate yet again across the valley all cower, including the tall leader who is resisting the invitation to single combat. As we overhear Saul's fighters discuss the frightening challenge offered by the Philistine giant the newcomer focuses on the notion of reward. A character's first direct discourse is typically diagnostic: Saul's first words spoke of turning back from a failed mission (9:5) while David here talks about reward, provoking the information from the others not once but twice. Rewards go only to victors, so the query signifies efficiently the difference between the two anointeds of YHWH. Saul seems, by contrast, inept,

---

[8] Polzin, *Samuel and the Deuteronomist* 155–56, 164–67.

[9] Some think that Goliath's unprotected spot is his forehead, others the back of his knees where his leggings have to permit him to walk.

[10] This second "first meeting" of David, and Saul's apparent confusion along the same lines at the end of this long chapter (17:55) tempt biblical scholars, not unreasonably, to suppose that the text has been spliced or redacted. Indeed, I agree that it has; but the job has been done artistically enough so that we see both the continuity and the seam. Almost Picasso-like, the storyteller gives us two first meetings of Saul and David, as though the moment is so important and the tradition so rich that we have to have at least two stories.

unable to do his job. If a giant urges single combat, to whom are his words addressed? Saul's job includes fighting Philistines. The narrator intensifies Saul's lack by reminding us that the taunting has been going on already for forty days; Saul is apparently stuck: not able to break off and leave, not able to pull himself together and go forward. Part of Saul's situation is surely that no one is helping him until, as before, his men bring the solution to the king's problems before him; so David's words are made known to Saul.

The verbal exchange between them (17:31-37) is instructive, especially if we are alert for reflections of Saul. David, challenged and countered by Saul on the basis of inexperience (not size, a topic Saul understandably does not raise), responds specifically to that point as he makes his case. Telling how his shepherd task has befitted him to fight hand to hand with lion and bear, to snatch sheep from their very jaws, David also theologizes, we might say.[11] That is, he characterizes the tall Philistine's demeanor as a challenge to YHWH—who, David now reveals, has been the shepherd boy's assistance prior to this moment. The point I want to stress here is the contrast not simply in confidence but in knowledge of God. Saul says little of God that inspires my sense that they are on intimate terms: he has so far shown himself not irreligious at all, but rather non-familiar with, non-intuitive about God. David, somehow, draws on a different fund of experience. What David seems to know already Saul will never learn. Saul and David are drawn such that David knows what Saul does not, detects in Goliath's scorn some insult to God, pushing us once again to see the two tall fighters as silhouettes of each other.

And so Saul summons David toward kingship by delegating to him the task of going before the people to fight Philistines. It is, along the lines I am developing, David's first tussle with Saul and will be quite definitive for both. But here we are shown another miniature of Saul's characterization as monarch(y), a *mise-en-abyme:* Saul clothes David in the royal armor, which David accepts briefly and then puts aside, refuses. At the surface, and in his discourse, he explains that the king's armor is too big for him, will hamper rather than help him. But we, watching, can see as well Saul giving David his royal identity and David refusing to take it from the proffered hand but rather earning it on his own terms. It can be another moment for us to register Saul's blindness, his lack of self-knowledge, as

---

[11] Alter, *David Story* 105–107, makes three helpful points: First, he uses "patriotic" for David's language, which I think is more nuanced than "religious" (while including it); second, he adds David's queries to three; and he points out that as David chatters, Saul is silent, having nothing to say.

he seems not to register any of these dynamics. We, standing outside of him, see what he is doing. The larger reading challenge is to stand both "in" and "outside" of ourselves and appropriate the result from both angles. The scene finishes well for the Israelite side: the giant with the armor and the arrogance crashes over, another fall of the mighty resembling Eli's descent (ch. 4), Dagan's tumbles (ch. 5), Agag's cutting down (ch. 15), and a preview of the end of the story we are reading (look ahead to ch. 31 if you wish). The leader dies alone, slain by his own sword, his head taken off his body, his armor claimed, his surviving men fled. It is another way of indicating that the first king—the monarchy itself—is prematurely dead, its demise rehearsed in detail long before it happens. Saul steps away from Goliath, as it were, and continues his reign, but we will remember what we have seen when our story finishes at chapter 31.

Saul (again) invites David to court and kingship (17:55–18:16)

But the narrator "rewinds the film" of this episode to show Saul watching David depart (the motif word "see" occurs again) for the encounter with the Philistine that has already been recounted. He asks, "Abner, whose son is this young man?" (17:55) and directs him to find out when Abner professes not to know. When David returns from battle Saul puts the question to him (v. 58). A rather amazing thing happens here: though narratively speaking David stands holding the dripping head of a man who has terrorized the whole group for many days, Saul does not allude to it at all but homes in on the question of sonship. And indeed, that topic seizes control: how Saul will make David a son and then seek to remove him. Saul's language again (recall twice in ch. 16, now at 18:2) moves to take David from Jesse and make him his own. David, who has three times called himself Saul's servant (17:32, 34, 36) now says in response (17:58): "I am the son of your servant Jesse of Bethlehem." In what first seems to be a parallel and reinforcing move Jonathan makes David a brother, even a twin, loving David as he (Jonathan) loves his very self. Like Saul, Jonathan divests himself of his royal accoutrements and gives them to David, who does not refuse this set (18:1-4).[12] But that David accepts Jonathan's gift but not Saul's also underlines tension and competitiveness

---

[12] There is some sense among commentators that Jonathan cedes his crown-princely position to David here: Alter, *David Story* 112, says that is what David accepts at least subliminally, with which concur Edelman, *Saul* 136; David Jobling, *1 Samuel* (Collegeville: The Liturgical Press, 1998) 93–99. See ibid. 111–15 for Jobling's sense of the importance of the father-son surrogacy theme.

here: that Jonathan makes David a brother does not quite make him Saul's son. Fathers and sons, dynastic sons, new sons continue to be central to our narrative.

A second moment that gives vast insight in proportion to its brevity is the victory song of women that greets the returning heroes (18:6-9). The verse of the song we hear comes in classic and compact Hebrew parallelism: verb/subject/object and then, verb omitted (carried from before), new subject, object magnified. Scholars are split as to the valence of the song, whether technically to put David second and with a larger unit is inevitably to show disrespect to Saul.[13] Since they cannot agree, let me offer this: That Saul construes it as negative is the important thing. However the women authored it, the king takes it over, revises it in his throat, blames the singers and the other sung hero, makes the recital more significant than the event it recounts. Besides listening in as Saul blames, we may also remark him failing to review who it was that allowed David to take on the Philistine, why David's help was required despite forty days of opportunities for Saul. Saul also now articulates to himself the dreaded thing: "What more can he have but the kingdom?" (18:8). It seems in the present context a big jump—granted we know he is not wrong. Even as they are returning from their "first" meeting, Saul turns against David. What Saul presumably most hates he brings into existence, even while resisting it. It is the manner of their relating that will absorb this story from now on.[14] What Saul dreads begins to shape his reality.

The narrator furnishes another bit of information that also testifies on multiple levels. The young musician who had come to soothe the king when the evil spirit constrained him is no longer able to do that job. Now (18:10-11) when David plays, Saul—pressed by the spirit—throws his spear toward the young man. Once again we hear Saul talk to himself: "I will pin David to the wall . . ." but it does not happen. Saul sees himself as powerful and skilled but makes visible, twice, that such is not the case. David eludes him twice, avoids "receiving" the king's weapons here as he did when facing Goliath. Saul's selftalk goes unreal in one sense, too real in another. Saul sees himself as a hunter, David as a quarry: warped portraits; before their dance is complete, the identifications will be apt but the tags reversed. The narrator summarizes that David is successful in everything

---

[13] We may think of thousands and ten thousands in terms of zeroes, but Hebrew numbers are not set up like that. What has been said is two units: thousands, myriads. There is an escalation, no doubt, but more subtle than it seems in English.

[14] Edelman, *Saul* 143, shrewdly poses the question: why is Saul so afraid of losing what he had already been assured is gone from him?

he is given to do (by Saul), the verb making a wordplay with language addressed to Saul by Samuel in 13:13. The same sound (different letter for s) articulates "acted foolishly" *(s[ɔ]kl)*, "succeeded" *(s[ʊ]kl)*.

Saul (twice) invites David into his family (18:17-30)

There is perhaps no better place to watch the king founder and flounder than when he involves his family in his struggle with David.[15] Saul has two daughters, Merab and Michal. He now works to make David his son-in-law through these two young women. The first episode is sketchy, gaining significance retrospectively as the second develops. Saul's first "proposal" is spoken directly to David and offered with a condition: fight YHWH's battles. David's rejoinder is similarly direct (by comparison with what lies just ahead!): "Who am I . . . that I should become son-in-law to the king?" (18:17-18). Saul's "outer" language is accompanied by inner discourse: "I will not raise a hand against him; let the Philistines deal with him," and David's question hands back both formal and thematic ambiguity to Saul, since it is not so clear how he has answered. Merab, of course, is not on the scene, and we are not perhaps surprised to learn that when the time comes to give her to David she is given to another. Questions abound here, but we must press on.

A rumor next makes its way to the king, as rumors do, perhaps most fecundly when their utterers anticipate what is desired. That is, Saul is brought information he desires, which sets in train this next episode in the "betrothals" of Saul's daughters and David. We, reading the rumor of Michal's love for David, may ask if it is true or false—not because we can know, but because our assumption (even if unreflected upon by ourselves) influences our interpretation.[16] The rumor works whether true or false; it pleases Saul, whether true or false. This time his selftalk comes first to us: we hear him refer to David in the third person and plan to make him a husband snared by his wife, a foe dealt with by Philistines. Saul's own role here is to launch the processes by means of the betrothal. We see Saul here envisioning unlikely outcomes. The Philistines will never lay a hand on

---

[15] I have written on "Michal material" several times; for further detail consult Barbara Green, *Mikhail Bakhtin and Biblical Scholarship: An Introduction* (Atlanta: Society of Biblical Literature Press, 2000) ch. 3, and "The Engaging Nuances of Genre: Reading Saul and Michal Afresh," in Carleen Mandolfo and Timothy Sandoval, eds., *Relating to the Text: Form-Critical and Interdisciplinary Insights Into the Bible* (Sheffield: Sheffield Academic Press, forthcoming).

[16] Also by way of assumptions inventory, ask yourself whether you think Saul knows that David is his replacement or not. The story is silent on the topic, so far; it is a reader's call.

David—rather the reverse. Saul is never successful in catalyzing them to do his work for him: again, to the contrary. Saul also conspicuously over-looks the previous engagement transaction that has aborted. Direct dis-course comes next—we can spot it in 18:21 because it addresses "you": "You shall now be my son-in-law." But it is more rehearsal than perfor-mance; Saul entrusts this proposal to servants to deliver for him. He tells them what else to say: pleasing to the king, popular with everyone else. Saul's discourse is doubled here in a variety of ways: we know he is saying one thing and planning another; he has borrowed David's phrasing from the previous scene; he is sending his words on the lips of others; and he is telling half-truths, in that "pleasing to the king" hardly exhausts Saul's complex relationship with David. Saul's language shows himself split along a number of risky paths.

Though we are not privy to the servants' version of the proposal we do get to read the message they bring back to Saul (presumably from David), which is itself suitably multivoiced: "Does it seem to you a little thing to become the king's son-in-law, seeing that I am a poor man and of no repute?" (18:24). Even quickly, we can hear a lot in this rejoinder. To summarize a few of the factors: First, it is the same[17] "regret" that David previously sent and that Saul seems to have accepted at face value. So David's sending it again underlines that this is round two between these two warriors over the daughters of Saul. David may be hinting that Saul al-ready showed him disrespect by accepting his first "no" without objection, or perhaps suggesting that the king is trifling with his unworthiness yet again. It strikes me as a rebuke in either case, granted its polite phrasing. Second, if we attend to the chatter that we heard at the Goliath scene David has already earned this royal prize and the negotiations ought not still be going on. Third, when David self-deprecates now, given all we know of his status, it may be a teasing of his overlord. Fourth, the language of "little" that constructs this response from David is linked with a series of word-plays running the length of this story that bring to our attention not just tall and short but heavy/honored and light/trifled-with that are themselves a whole discourse. Fifth, if these two have an ongoing struggle over whose son David is, his claim to be of no account is not very filial. Sixth, David sends Saul's wording back, arguably at cross-purposes with the senders' use. Finally, seventh, by answering with a question David has not actually made clear whether he is saying yes or no, but is pushing Saul to make the choice.

---

[17] It is not quite *verbatim*, but close.

And so Saul reads a "yes," names a price that David pays, readily and double (18:25-27). As the scene ends Saul has a new son-in-law where it appears to me that he wanted David's tombstone. The narrator announces Saul's insight by the end of the piece: he has been ganged up on or outmaneuvered, by God's spirit-with-David and by his daughter's love for that young man, if not as well by David's skill. Saul's sense of himself as manager of the snare for David arguably takes a hit, and Saul is the more afraid by negotiation's end (18:28). The conclusion of the unit is rhetorically uncertain, but were we to follow it to the end of the chapter we learn two more crucial pieces of information: first that the Philistines, far from countering David as Saul had supposed and planned, are bested by him continuously; that David's fame increases (in what is most usually understood as a zero-sum game)—i.e., Saul's and David's fame will vary inversely (not likely to please Saul). And most important, though not with total clarity (only pronouns and adjectives occur in Hebrew, no names), the narrator says Saul was David's enemy from that day on (v. 29). So a major corner has been turned as a result of this "construction project": gain for some, loss for some, both transactions managed by both players. It is an amazing gain in Saul's characterization from so brief a unit.

Saul's children choose (again) between kings (19:1-17)

Saul's plan to kill David (always said in Hebrew somewhat impersonally by Saul, as if to avoid naming himself as subject of a verb can buffer the reality) becomes more overt. Jonathan names to David that Saul is "seeking him" and bids David hide while Jonathan intervenes with the father. The intervention is successful, apparently: "Saul heeded the voice of Jonathan: Saul swore: 'As the LORD lives, he will not be put to death'" (19:6). Three things may catch our ear here. First, as Jonathan speaks to Saul his words are duplex in a new set of ways. Jonathan has two clients; he tells his father's quarry to take care while Jonathan intervenes. Such secrecy is not neutral. Second, Jonathan urges his father not to wrong a man who has done only "good" to him—again that freighted word that recalls to us, and should to Saul, the prophetic descriptor of Saul's royal replacement (15:28). The things Jonathan labels as good are the very things that seem to pain Saul. He did your job for you when you could not cope with it, Jonathan urges. This sort of soothing tends to enflame, whether the speaker so intends or not. Third, Jonathan's reminder that Saul rejoiced redirects us to recall that the king's joy was totally missing from the scene.[18]

---

[18] Fokkelman, *Fates* 210–14, notes that at a moment of rejoicing, Saul is angry.

Saul was angered by the event and set against David as others rejoiced. But by the time this intervention is over Jonathan has shown his loyalties once again, even if we suppose that he has done a service both to his father and to David. The narrator evaluates that things went back to what they were before (19:7). What was it like between Saul and David before, we ask, remembering that from the return from the battlefield itself it has been contentious. And, sure enough, we learn that, as before (18:10-11), Saul hurls his spear at David. So Saul's dreadful ambivalence—his bungling of and backpedaling on life and death[19]—gets another bout of exercise. His words are shown to be unstable; his recent oath is rendered void, as we saw when the life of Jonathan was at stake. Saul swivels from his goal of David's death only briefly before returning to his obsession in regard to it. And now Saul has driven David a bit farther away, making the chase more of a challenge mostly to himself.

We follow David from the palace to the house he and Michal share, Saul's men in pursuit. The king's exposed animus against David features in a final scene between Saul and Michal (19:11-17), where once again their discourse is amenable to Bakhtin's insights. Since in the betrothal scene between Saul and David Michal was silent if not absent, let me summarize her role there so we may note something different in this encounter: Saul made Michal (as did other characters and the narrator) an exchangeable possession between powerful men, a token for servants to barter between those men. Michal was assigned by Saul to be ally of the dread enemy of her people and a snare to her husband—also incidentally opponent of her father, in the event. Since Michal was not present except as others spoke of her she abetted the moves of neither Saul nor David. If, with Bakhtin, we demote the "omniscient narrator" and promote both our own readerly scrutiny and the centrifugal interplay of all the language, we discover that it was not her self-confessed love for David that initiated all this action but the anonymous rumor floated to her father and his acting upon it. There is no basis for any absolute knowledge that Michal loves David. All subsequent readings that rise from that taproot, ramified however creatively, must be reexamined and mostly abandoned.[20]

This scene is woven by threads of five direct discourse utterances. Michal informs a silent David: "If you do not save your life tonight,

---

[19] Fokkelman, *Fates* 248, 257.

[20] Wonderfully useful is an anthology of David J. A. Clines and Tamara C. Eskenazi, eds., *Telling Queen Michal's Story: An Experiment in Comparative Interpretation* (Sheffield: JSOT Press, 1991), which brings between two covers a whole set of relevant commentary on the Michal texts. To browse those materials is to rethink what exactly any of us thinks we are doing as we read and interpret.

tomorrow you will be killed" (19:11). She picks up correctly on what the narrator has just said: Saul has sent messengers to kill David in the morning. She sides with husband over father here, thwarting the one to save the other; or does she thwart herself to save both, thwart both to save herself? Her speech is a variant of her brother Jonathan's in 19:2, but more succinct, and urging escape instead of hiding, noting that the morning will bring death, not reconciliation. Michal's initiative lets David out the window to escape from Saul. To assist one is to resist the other, commentators allege. But her action need not be simply one of those *or* the other; she may have other motives we can factor in, should we resist the construction of her love of David, which we have not heard from her. Simultaneously she helps him away from her, losing him, as some would say, or perhaps loosing him out of her life. Flee tonight or die tomorrow, she says to him, and he, silent, obeys. Michal is the agent here, and David, though silent and assisted, is surely active on his own behalf as well, making haste on foot as she verbally buys time.

Michal says to Saul's dispatched but wordless messengers (who are beginning to abound, their presence testifying both to power and weakness), "He is sick." The effective strategy is delay, as the messengers go back for instructions. Michal is enigmatic and opaque, her words spacious. Saul rejoins, "Lift him on the bed to me to kill him," (19:14, author's translation). As before, the agent of the killing remains unspecified in Saul's mouth. Michal's deception with the bedclothes is evidently discovered before the bed is brought to Saul, who instead of a bedded image receives a report to which we hear only a sentence of response. Saul says to Michal, "Why have you deceived[21] me like this and let my enemy go, so that he has escaped?" (19:17). Saul draws his others only in relation to his own desire to remain king. The man in question is "my enemy," not any of the other descriptors that might suit the scene from another angle. Typically, Saul does not voice his own role but blames the other. Michal responds to Saul, "He said to me, 'Let me go; why should I kill you?'" She quotes something we did not hear, perhaps making it up, giving truth to Saul's accusation that she has deceived him, not with a dummy but with language. Alternatively, David may have said it. The peculiarly Hebrew causative construction suggests yet another possibility: why should I be the cause of your dying? An accusation thus emerges: Saul is drawn as potential killer of his daughter to get his enemy. To shed innocent blood is what she has prevented him from doing here, though she does not say it. Perhaps some of the blood she saves is her own. The warning of the elders that a king would take sons and

---

[21] He uses the same word as when accusing his fighters (14:33); it will recur in 28:12.

daughters (8:11-13) is beginning to accrue a dreadful significance, as Saul loses to at least some extent the loyalty of these two of his to the son he took from Jesse.

Yʜᴡʜ's *spirit opposes Saul's resistance (19:18-24)*

This last section, detailing the flight of David and Saul's questing determination to thwart it, shows us two things beyond its main communication, which is that Saul failed while trying mightily. The first is that this scene, unlike the preceding six, is not in any clear sense shown from the inner view of anyone; conversation is lacking. Second, I suggest that Saul's energy to get at David is now matched by the shifted position of the spirit that once was Saul's helper (10:9-13; 11:6). The agency of the spirit, visible primarily in its effect, was never Saul's own but his helper in the task of being king. Once he is replaced, and especially insofar as he refuses to go and turns on his replacement, God's spirit must oppose Saul's lethal determination. Here it throws him to the ground where we see him lie, naked and alone, acting-the-prophet (whatever that means), generating comment from observers as before. We are not privy to the spirit's communication with Saul, see only that by the end of the scene Saul calls off for the moment (has been talked out of?) his pursuit of David and returns home. A note: Yesterday I sat at a coffee shop, near a window through which I watched a homeless man arrange a blanket for himself and a dog, eventually settling them outside my gaze except if I leaned uncomfortably across my table to look. A grandfather came by with two children around the age of three, who were immediately drawn to the dog; I could not see why they were so interested, but I watched each of them fascinated and in some communication with Grandpa, their attention riveted toward the dog. The little girl finally turned away, but the boy did not and had to be picked up bodily and talked at by the grandfather. The child went limp, kicked, shook his head, tried to squirm free, squalled, and was eventually manhandled away from the dog—distracted if not convinced. Saul seems distracted for the moment from his pursuit of David.

Conclusion

Saul determined to stay king no matter what, Saul at cross-purposes with God, is losing sight of the "one thing needful," distracted from performing his other responsibilities, notably from fighting Philistines. Saul's verbal edges are linking poorly with his "others." He seems conflicted and in denial as he plans, blames, alibis, pretends. His character is drawn not without sympathy by the storyteller and constructed compassionately, I hope, in this book. Saul offers me—us—a lot by the honesty of the portrayal and thus invites us to intersect imaginatively with the complexities set forth here. Though we have read these chapters and their discourse primarily at the human level, they continue to work at the institutional and political-social level as a riddle, especially in their intense communication about the deadliness of dynastic sons. We may still have our money on Jonathan, despite all we have witnessed, or we may have some confidence that David can do well, especially if we overlook the Elide sons, the new boy at the Shiloh shrine who also begets renegades; if there is ever a group of sons that goes out of control, it will be David's. Shall the return from exile be with Saulide sons? With Davidic kings? With royal sons at all? The picture of Saul lying naked, isolated, resisting but thwarted by the spirit of God speaks plainly at least to me.

CHAPTER SIX

Futile Searching (1 Samuel 20–23)

"What shall we think about a text that can do its work only by making its central character insane? Is it kingship itself that is insane?"

David Jobling, *1 Samuel*

─────────────

We are all familiar, I suspect, with the phenomenon of entrapment. Though its most prominent instances may be the "stings" of law enforcement, where those suspected of nefarious temptations are given opportunities to participate in staged versions of them, we could all follow ourselves through a normal day and find a number of similar if less dramatic encounters. Friends may urge us to go out at night instead of study, and we—not unwilling to be persuaded—are nonetheless a bit shocked to hear ourselves blamed for being the enticer when the matter arises that evening in our circle of friends. Who was asker and who asked? Why was *I*, library-bound, urged to detour to a coffee house while others moved relentlessly and undistracted toward the stacks and carrels? Or we may find ourselves in some kind of a negative relationship where, though our desires are conflicted, we signal some kind of willingness to participate that is taken as consent and we are blamed—even hold ourselves responsible—for some outcome. Who lays the bait, who swallows it? Can it be mere chance that all my relationships tend in this same direction? Who is the pursuer, who the pursued? The point is that many, even most of our transactions are complex in this way—are dialogical, Bakhtin would say. We must acknowledge our inevitable relatedness as we make our moves in whatever venue.

In the next seven chapters of 1 Samuel (20–26) and in the next two chapters of this book we will interpret the entrapment dynamic between Saul and others. The complexity of discourses will be the best place to hear it; in fact, the discourses are crafted so that we will not fail to pick up on the many ways in which Saul is both connecting and failing to catch with all those around him. He will, for the most part, refuse to answer for his own part in his relationships (whatever we may detect in his patterns), consequently driving all of his partners from him. Saul is like a man going deaf: He hates the thought and denies it, refuses the help others would offer while blaming them for talking too softly; he makes himself difficult to be around, with the result that his friends avoid him, and he grows all the lonelier and crustier to those who still do come near—until they drop off as well. Saul's refusal to accept the termination of his rule sows devastation that continues to unfold from his refusal to answer for what he has been told; it hobbles him increasingly, and others as well. He articulates brief moments of self-knowledge that—though quickly submerged—are key for our own transformative reading of ourselves and our relationships, especially with God, who also tends to speak softly. We will have occasion to revisit the riddle genre and add to our sense of what we are being told about the madness of monarchy as we see some mad monarchs.

My thesis is that Saul is tempted out in pursuit of David by the planning of the younger man, who sets up a "sting" in which Saul colludes. Saul shows little evidence of being conscious of what is happening, no sense that his fears and denials make him easy to "play." His complicity has already been sketched for us in his inviting David to his palace, arming him to slay the Philistine, betrothing him to his daughter, and so forth. Saul exhibits (so far) no recognition of his own deepest vulnerability, no loophole through which he might slip to be other-than-king. He is so identified with his role—coincident with it—that he cannot engage God, who has fired him from that responsibility. Saul has over-identified with a role now forbidden to him; hence he and God have no grounds for conversation. Kingship, now if not before, is bad for Saul's health in several ways. The entrapment that develops here hardens Saul against alternatives. There is evidence—meager but visible—that Saul has it in him to do better than pursue and be pursued by David. But he is caught. We will handle our material in three steps: first, a long piece that interlinks Saul with his two "sons," David and Jonathan (1 Samuel 20); second, an episode where Saul's alienation from his own kin, from his priests, and from God becomes painfully obvious (chs. 21–22); and finally a sketched scenario where we can see that David's bait has been picked up and Saul has moved into the pursuit game that will continue to absorb all his energies (ch. 23).

Two sons plan for their father (1 Samuel 20)

This long chapter is filled with pairs of verbal exchanges: fifteen of them. If you turned in such a composition as part of a drama or novel I suspect it would be blue-penciled for tightening up! We will move through this gallery of verbal encounters, lingering just long enough to observe the artistic lines underlying the sketches of Saul and to watch their cumulative impact as David flees Saul's palace permanently. In the first section we can imagine the two "sons" scratching drawings of the "father" in the dust as they plan, effacing previous ones as they proceed but leaving quite a lasting impression in the memories of readers. I will touch quickly the six rounds of their discussion (20:1-21), leaving you to etch more detail as it strikes you. David begins (v. 1) by reusing his old question from 17:29 (also asked of Saul by Jonathan in 19:4-5) to sketch Saul as unfairly in pursuit of him. This is a good place to check your own reaction: Do you instinctively answer David's questions to Jonathan, ". . . what is my sin against your father that he is trying to take my life?" with a list of instances where it is undeniably true that Saul is after David? or with a rush of apologetics for the beleaguered monarch? Neither view can knock out the other; the point to diagnose is your own reaction. Our examen sensitizes us to Jonathan's response (v. 2), which comes in rapid rebuttal to David's first drawing of Saul as malicious or irrational. Underlying Jonathan's alteration to David's portrait is his insistence that his bond with his father is such that, if Jonathan does not recognize what David says, it cannot be so. Father cannot have a plan that son does not know. Jonathan's first sketch here includes himself, close to his father. We may think his verbosity a bit defensive![1]

David rejoins (round two, v. 3) by tactfully, strategically skirting the portrait of the father and son as knowing each others' hearts. He shifts to account for Jonathan's ignorance by saying his father does not want to grieve Jonathan, but David insists that Saul's pursuit is indeed lethal.[2] David's friend, Saul's son, seems to abandon (quickly?) his first drawing to accept what David has just shown him: a murderous man with whom they must cope (v. 4). In round three (vv. 5-9) David skillfully capitalizes on the sense of the father and son as close but also on his own ties with Jonathan to devise a diagnostic test at the king's table. David hands Jonathan a

---

[1] Robert M. Polzin, *Samuel and the Deuteronomist: A Literary Study of the Deuteronomic History: I Samuel* (San Francisco: Harper & Row, 1989)187–90, is helpful in his discussion of characterization here, smoothing out some of the more frequently-cited inconsistencies in behaviors.

[2] Polzin, *Samuel and the Deuteronomist* 190–96, shows Jonathan suggestible in his naïveté.

speech to make, which anticipates two possible responses for Saul. David says, in effect: Here is the king at table with you, while my place is empty; see how he reacts: if he approves my absence with a "Good," fine,[3] but if not. . . . As you may remember, "good" is by now a very loaded word, linked to the "better man" with whom Saul is to be replaced and hovering around David in all the adulation he has picked up from his deeds at court. The chances of Saul's approving David with this word seem small indeed. We move closer to entrapment here, not only for Saul but for Jonathan as well, whose response now contradicts the picture of paternal-filial intimacy that he just drew: If I knew that my father wished you ill, would I not tell you? Jonathan, we may think, is both manipulating and manipulated. Will this plan reveal or precipitate Saul's state?

Their round four (vv. 10-11) rehearses details, the two moving away from their first meeting site to continue planning. In their fifth exchange (vv. 12-17) Jonathan makes three condition- and oath-laden promises to David, reinforcing his wordless utterance of fealty when he first saw David (18:1, 3-4) and implicating YHWH to cut off the enemies of David. Whether Jonathan intends or anticipates it or not, the "fall guy" of such language is his own father. Their final (sixth) exchange here (vv. 18-23), though ostensibly rehearsing the mode for the next communication, also seems to presume in its careful subterfuge that the king will *not* have reacted well and that secrecy and codes will be required. Jonathan has moved some way from his initial "impossible!" and is now apparently fully drawn into David's plan. Though David does not speak here, as we look at the drawing of the king with which their planning includes, the authorial signature I see on it is David's.

The next series of conversations occurs at the feast, as planned. The narrator interjects (vv. 24-26) to "set the table" for us, Saul's celebration where David's place is conspicuously empty when it ought have been filled. Since we have already been given that information I sense here the narrator underlining the importance of what we are about to witness: Saul watches the absent David, watched by Jonathan, overseen by David. The next exchange (our seventh—v. 26) is Saul's own: his proffered excuse— uttered twice—makes clear what silent question prompted it; reiteration betrays the depth of Saul's feeling, whatever particular emotional blossom is about to bud. When a second night's feast makes the lack of David prominent once again, Saul cannot restrain his speech and it emerges in a question to Jonathan (round eight, vv. 27-29) about "the son of Jesse."

---

[3] Polzin, *Samuel and the Deuteronomist* 188–92, raises the "rational" question of why these two would continue to believe Saul even if he were to give his word again.

Commentators hear the sobriquet as dismissive, which seems likely in context; I hear it also as germane to the whole point under discussion: whose son is David? Saul's question now, flushed from the underbrush of his self-talk, reveals the inadequacy of his own previous effort to convince himself that David's absence roots in temporary uncleanness, since he backs up to rescrutinize the previous evening. That he is correct to doubt the excuse offered does not alter much the portrait of the king, chased at least partly by his own denial into this thicket of testing woven by David and Jonathan. Saul's question evokes now from Jonathan the words David had given him to say, with minor shifts. The mix of reporting language (Jonathan's own words) with reported speech (quoting David to speak in the first person) makes audible two things: first, the choice of David to celebrate with his father Jesse's household, and second, the collusion between the two young men over against the king.

If the ninth round (vv. 30-34) seems all too familiar, it is perhaps because we remember previous scenes like it, where Saul, Jonathan, and David have had this "same" conversation; or subconsciously we have filled out the alternative to Saul's "Good!" left unspecified by the two planners. Saul, prodded, reacts. Saul, readily reactive, invites prodding. His anger is directed not unsuitably against Jonathan. He slurs him and indirectly his birth.[4] In one of his most candid reflections so far Saul tells Jonathan that he knows that his son is choosing Jesse's son over against his own lineage. Of course, from another angle the reference to "Jonathan's kingdom" denies the information Saul was given so unequivocally by Samuel in 13:13-14 and 15:26. There is to be no kingdom for Jonathan, no matter the efforts of any. So Saul's candor here, if sincere and an improvement, remains nonetheless unreal. Then, as if his blunt detailing of realities might convince his son, Saul again demands that Jonathan send David not to his father's table, but to Saul to be killed. Jonathan's response to the paternal outburst defies that fatherly edict and echoes both his own and David's earlier language (19:4; 20:1): "'Why should he be put to death? What has he done?'" If previously (19:4-7) Jonathan's intervention dissuaded Saul from pursuit, now the effect goes contrary. Resistance to what Saul has

---

[4] Jan P. Fokkelman, *Narrative Art and Poetry in the Books of Samuel: Volume II: The Crossing Fates* (Assen, The Netherlands: Van Gorcum, 1986) suggests the slur is not directed against Jonathan's mother *per se* but conveys the notion that the son is congenitally flawed (p. 334). That may be so, though contemporary feminist theory will not so easily overlook the manner of derogation, nor will a Bakhtinian reader miss the positioning of the old conflict of sons and their parentage. For a more gender-sensitive interpretation consult David Jobling, *1 Samuel* (Collegeville: The Liturgical Press, 1998) 178.

been told is God's choice drives Saul's actions. Saul's wordless response (vv. 32-34) is to confirm what he hates, the conflation of the two "sons," as he hurls the spear formerly aimed at David now toward Jonathan. The long arc, rising when we were told that Jonathan loved David as another self, descends as we watch Saul's spear hurtling toward Jonathan. And now not one but two sons are conspicuously missing from the table as Jonathan leaves, grieving for David; the narrator, with clever ambiguity (avoiding proper names), says his father had shamed him.

Before concluding with the flurry of arrows that brings the two artists together for the penultimate encounter between them that we are to witness, let us add up what we have seen. David's drawing of Saul as murderous has been confirmed by the king himself. Jonathan's sense of being in the counsel of his father is ironically confirmed as well, since he now indeed shares the burden of what is in his father's heart. Whether you think Saul has been entrapped unfairly or simply made to place his cards on the table is yours to judge. What I will say here, partly by anticipation, is that Saul, even cornered, does not kill David, the many threats notwithstanding. So these drawings are right in some senses, wrong in others. Whether other plans laid by these two might have authored Saul differently is a matter for speculation. But in any case the two young men converse again in five more elliptical and enigmatic rounds (vv. 35-43) that give us not so much realism as a stress on the representational aspect of this chapter. Jonathan's speech is double in a new way as he directs it ostensibly to his servant— who is managing his weapons, we may observe—though more intensely to his covenant brother to whom he already entrusted his gear (and likely his position). David is thus directed to run, is affirmed to be sent by God, is urged to hurry (vv. 35-39). Jonathan's words stress that YHWH is with David and make tangible as well their mutual commitment to each other's heirs (vv. 40-42).

The trail is laid (1 Samuel 21–22)

Though we could be distracted here by David—and we would not be the first to abandon Saul for the younger man—we will stay resolutely fixed on the old king as David now lays a wide and obvious trail for Saul to take. It has several phases, though a common objective, as I observe it and invite you to ponder it: to lure the incumbent king away from his own familiars—such as they are—in pursuit of his quarry. There are three sets of moments for us: David with the Elide priests of Nob, David with the Philistine king Achish and the nameless king of Moab, and finally the culmination of these efforts as Saul "loses it" and alienates his own supporters.

David flees first to Nob, where he engages the Elide priest Ahimelech (21:1-9). The fugitive's requests include food and, almost incidentally, weaponry.[5] My reading here is that David's language—specifically his use of "the king," which we know refers now to himself as well as Saul—misrepresents the situation he describes to the priest.[6] As a result of this very odd encounter where David claims the only food on site[7] (the bread of presence) and the only weapon (Goliath's sword)—a request that necessitates the priest handling the ephod within the purview of one of Saul's men (Doeg) —the priest will be compromised. David lays groundwork for an encounter that will lead to the death of Saul's priests and to his losing of access to God through them, paltry though it has been. It is a violation Saul will scarcely be able to ignore, once it is called to his attention by the man who watched it. Motives we will not be able to sort out, but the visual trail is clear.

David's second egregious bait involves flight (with the Philistine Goliath's sword) to the Philistine king[8] Achish of Gath (21:10-15). And while weighing the import of this move, which would seem to compromise all that David has done so far in terms of opposing the Philistines, we must remain focused upon the scene's contribution to Saul's characterization. David, Philistine slayer *par excellence,* risks provoking the Philistine king by moving into his territory. Other Philistines recognize David, call him king of the land, and hum the bars of the song the women sang after the Goliath slaying. David feigns madness once his cover is penetrated, disguising himself with insanity. Is "the king" mad? How will "the king" respond to the presence in his court of the slayer of Goliath, carrying the sword, no less? Achish picks up on what he sees—David's scribbling and dribbling—and dismisses what he has been told. Do I lack madmen, he rejoins, that you bring another into my presence, into my house?!

---

[5] David's encounter with the priest is made additionally complex (for Christian readers) since Jesus comments on it in the synoptic gospels, thereby encrusting it not inappropriately but confusingly with another context that seems to override its "original" one. See Mark 2:25-26; Matt 12:3-4; Luke 6:3-4.

[6] See Polzin, *Samuel and the Deuteronomist* 194–98, for his sense that David's language is deceptively simple, not simply deceptive.

[7] Fokkelman, *Fates* 352, points out how unlikely the scene is. He also notes that David brought five loaves (the same number under negotiation here) to the king's forces in ch. 17 and now in effect takes them back; an equivalent case may be made for the sword. Diana Edelman, *King Saul in the Historiography of Judah* (Sheffield: Sheffield Academic Press, 1991)164–67, who also thinks the focus of the unit is on the sword and not the food, notes the similarity of the phrasing to 10:4.

[8] Ralph W. Klein, *1 Samuel* (Waco: Word Books, 1983) 216, notes that it is unusual to call a Philistine leader a king rather than the more specific title for Philistine leaders. In the present context it underlines the unusual presence of five kings in a small space of reference.

David and Achish enact a series of royal caricatures, catching certain aspects of Saul, who also reacted naïvely to David's new presence in his court. Achish's strange discourse shows a raveled edge of Saul in relief. Achish, with ample cause to fear David, overlooks, underestimates him; and David allows it, for the moment. David's being praised to Achish does not provoke the Philistine ruler as perhaps we think it ought to have done. On the contrary, the narrator suggests, David fears Achish and makes himself appear harmless. The discourse rehearses for readers the identity of the king of the land, the madness of the king. Madness provides a loophole for David here, a means for him to evade a situation dangerous and compromising. We have, arguably, another *mise-en-abyme,* the faceoff of two kings: one feigning madness and the other taken in; one of them shrewd, one clueless; one residually powerful, one wily. But who plays each of those roles is for the reader to sort out.[9] Achish is a cipher for Saul, whom David taunts by his presence though he slips away, having baited his trap. Less developed is the odd moment where David presents himself at the Moabite court (22:1-5). Having attracted to himself some from his own father's house as well as others with miscellaneous grievances, David becomes their "captain." Seeking sanctuary for his parents in that transjordan land of his ancestors,[10] he himself is advised by his prophet Gad to go back to the land of Judah. David is laying a wide and obvious trail—to which Saul has not yet reacted.

But now he does. The last moment to be scrutinized in this middle section (22:6-23) continues the engagement of David with the priests of Nob. In fact this scene flows directly from what we have just observed, insofar as we have now not a king feigning madness but one who seems to have arrived at that unenviable state. This is, perhaps, Saul's worst moment, surely one of his least answerable acts. Our narrative storyline left Saul seething at his own festal table, having driven both of his sons from it—not least by hurling his spear at "them." The link back to Saul from David's recent exploits is made by the narrator, who observes that Saul hears now that David's local whereabouts (in the stronghold of Adullam) are known. Besides making a join so that the action can move forward, the narrator initiates a series of searches by Saul based on information he receives about the whereabouts of his quarry (chs. 23–26). Saul does

---

[9] Jobling, *1 Samuel* 212, observes that the Philistines in 1 Samuel are quite significant in organizing the action of the book. Of this particular encounter between David and Achish, Jobling suggests (p. 241) that Achish is made gullible here so that we will think that of him later.

[10] The book of Ruth makes its named heroine a Moabite and mother of David's ancestor.

not go after David here but first after the priests who seem to have abetted him.

We see Saul presiding at Gibeah, seated under a tamarisk tree, spear in hand, surrounded by his servants. The visual language of Saul's posture evokes in our mind's eye the ever-seated Eli (seated until he crashes over); and the king's grasping his spear recalls for us the occasions when he has hurled it, missing his target in each case—so another motif of failure.[11] Saul's direct discourse here shows, additionally, a deterioration in the relationship with his men from what we saw in chapters 16 and even 18, when his servants seemed concerned for his welfare and willing to carry out his wishes (granted, it was their concern that brought David to court!); it recalls more closely the atmosphere of chapters 19–21 when Saul's household is obviously at odds over David. Saul's words (22:7-8), addressed specifically to his fellow Benjaminites, accuse and envision circumstances where the "son of Jesse" will distribute valuable property and commissions to Saul's men. As is typically true of accusations, attention is drawn to more than the speaker may have intended. Saul's accusation is tangled, confused, rambling. He pictures these (hypothetical) bribes as payments for his own men's conspiracy of silence—specifically about the pact between Jonathan and David. His men's lack of sorrow on the king's behalf, Saul seems to imply, prevented them from disclosing to him information that Saul says has resulted in Jonathan's stirring up David to lie in wait for him. The accusation is complex, its main elements being the conspiratorial silence of his own men that prevents them from telling the king that David—thanks to Jonathan—is lying in wait for Saul.

The circuitous accusation, generating loud silence from the Benjaminites, relinks us back to the custom or justice of the king spoken out by the prophet Samuel when the people asked for a king (8:10-18, specifically vv. 12 and 14), which includes rewards for loyal service. But the issue here of who is distributing the rewards is less crucial than to whom, for what services, and with what result. Saul's talk here of hundreds and thousands may evoke the victory song of the women, which both he and the Philistines interpreted to Saul's disadvantage. Saul's charge of a conspiring between David and Jonathan makes present once again all the complex dealings between those two, which not only flushed Saul's fear of their bond out into the open but perhaps added to it. Whether there is evidence

---

[11] P. Kyle McCarter, *1 Samuel. A New Translation with Introduction and Commentary* (Garden City, N.Y.: Doubleday, 1980) 363, reports that the king seated in council under a sacred tree is a stock scene in Northwest Semitic art. His position under a tamarisk tree—the eventual site of Saul's burial—offers another proleptic reiteration of monarchic demise.

of David bestowing fields, vineyards, and commissions is dubious so far, yet shortly he will be providing booty and payment for those who have gathered around him (chs. 25, 27, 29, and 30). So Saul's charge is largely true. Saul faults his men for withholding information, which in fact he knows. Who has told Saul of the pact between David and Jonathan? Saul is desperate to know their doings. Has he imagined it? If so, again he is not incorrect. The explanation offered so frequently that Saul is paranoid over-looks and hence fails to mine this key piece of information that he gener-ates: David does lie in wait for Saul, thanks to the connivance of Jonathan and the silence of the king's own men—which Saul calls, perhaps harshly, conspiracy. Though Saul sounds mad to many in this outburst—an impres-sion reinforced by his subsequent action regarding the priests—the provo-cation is intense.[12]

In any case the only verbal response Saul generates is from Doeg, who reports that the son of Jesse came to the priest Ahimelech at Nob, that the priest inquired (of God) for him, giving him provisions and Goliath's sword. Since the narrator positioned Doeg between the food and weapons transactions we can reasonably understand that Doeg's narrative purpose is to bear witness to those events. Doeg slides comfortably into the groove of Saul's desire, using the disparaging patronym for David and exposing the deed of the priest.[13] That Doeg is quick to please the king seems patent, especially over against the silence of the Benjaminites, who may be imag-ined as eager not to *dis*please him. That part of what he says is factually true is also clear; even the charge that the priest helped David inquire of God (the manner of it is left unspecified) may be a report of what Doeg saw. And yet Doeg looks suspect here, I think, because of his obvious will-ingness to provide information that is about to be lethal. Once the foreigner has spoken, Saul summons not only the one priest but the whole line: Elides, their names suggest. Saul addresses the priest in the same non-respectful and accusatory way that he refers to David, underscoring by the patronym the dynastic elements of our story. Saul's charge is similar to what we just heard above, adding the priest to a list that includes David, Jonathan, and Saul's men. The crime is specified: the giving of bread and sword and the inquiry that has allowed David to escape and now lie in wait for Saul. That is, Saul takes Doeg's information and resets it in a larger context, makes the priest guilty of conspiracy by provisioning and inquir-ing for the fugitive and for failing to notify the king of the young man's

[12] Edelman, *Saul* 174, points out that Saul talks with the old vocabulary of 8:21; 9:15; 20:2; 13:13.

[13] Edelman, *Saul* 165.

flight—with the result that David lies in wait for Saul (22:13). Saul registers a feeling of being besieged—or stalked—by David. Part of what is being discoursed here is who is pursuing whom. The silence of the Benjaminites, the bluster of the Edomite, and the naïve objections of the Elide—not to mention Saul's outrageous revenge—conspire to mute the impact of Saul's insight on readers. But his intuition is close to the mark.

Ahimelech answers (22:14-15) somewhat in the mode of Jonathan in 19:1-7, saying exactly the wrong thing.[14] The priest praises David as faithful, characterizes him as royal son-in-law, honored in Saul's house. However it fits in with our readers' information, I think we must concede that there is no indication of any but a sincere answer here. The priest, somewhat in the manner of Saul's own familiars in chapter 16, seems ready to trust the king with honest information, however awkward it might potentially be. What strikes me, more than the disjunction of the priest's angle, is my own slowness to notice more readily that the priest's encomium no longer fit its object. David's behavior with the priest (at least) has vitiated that set of sacerdotal compliments. More faithful than all, turning aside to do Saul's work, honored in Saul's house—David seems no longer working to achieve any of this. That Ahimelech's sketch of David is vastly at odds with the construction Saul has just rendered is not a good sign, though of course the priest has no way of knowing the recent "conversation" between Saul and his men.

Though Saul cedes the giving of food and the sword without blame, the inquiry is a different matter. Saul, as we have seen consistently, has a weakness here in that he is unable to get unequivocal information from God, and of course is not willing to accept the information that does come to him bluntly. More than conspiracy, the inquiry charge strikes at a weakness of Saul—whose very name is to inquire. The priest, again disingenuously, does not answer directly the charge of inquiring for David, but ambiguously and foolishly says that if he inquired it is not the first time.[15] Did he inquire? Saul has only Doeg's word for it, Doeg whom we watched see the priest move the ephod to get at the sword. Can a foreigner have mistaken such a move for an inquiry? In any case Saul waits for no further information, but calls for the death of not only Ahimelech but the whole house of Elide priests. The elimination of not simply one priest but a whole

---

[14] Edelman also sees the resonance with the questioning of Jonathan in 14:43 (*Saul* 177).

[15] Commentators split over whether Ahimelech did or did not consult and over whether he does or does not say so. The point, rather, is that he is a doomed witness, a witness whose information is at odds with other things that we know.

group with their wives and livestock distracts somewhat from the actual issue at hand. The royal command, given ineffectually to those standing around him, brings to visibility Saul's general accusation that his men are disloyal to him. Though they refuse to obey the king, neither does any of those in attendance stop Doeg the Edomite from his task of slaughtering priests (nor, apparently, do the Elides resist). That his men refuse the order underlines both its egregiousness and Saul's inability to command his men.[16] Only Doeg is willing to obey, and he, the narrator says, using the technical language of the ban (which we heard in ch. 15), executes eighty-five priests, plus women, children, and domesticated animals. If, as Edelman hints, the herdsman Doeg is able to resemble both David and Saul we can see here a peculiar character of monarchy: dangerous to the priesthood.

That this narrative, with its lone escapee, connects to a prophecy delivered by a man of God (2:27-36), words which will be filled in full, incrementally, as the story proceeds, does not excuse Saul from his deed. Saul executes the priests not for the sins decried by the man of God but for appearing to side with David over against Saul. By its technical language the episode provokes recollection of Saul's own failure to execute the Amalekites when charged to do so, such that someone had to complete that task for him as well. And here, as there, the slaughter does not undo the failure to which it reacts. Saul has compounded his isolation from God by closing down priestly inquiry and allowing a lone survivor to escape into the camp of David.[17] Saul's action here, whatever else must be said about it, is counterproductive. What he most needs—information—he drives off; what he most fears—disloyalty—he invites. Saul will become ever more isolated in his quest to get the information he needs. Ahimelech has not responded to the satisfaction of all, and yet he is quickly mowed down rather than questioned at greater length.

More futile searching (1 Samuel 23)

If, as I have been suggesting, this whole portion of the story functions to detail the entrapment of the old king, Saul has now been provoked not only to see his priests slain by an Edomite while his own men stand resistant to a royal order, but also now to marshal his energies to track David instead of the foes of the people. If, as we recall, one of the purposes of hir-

---

[16] Fokkelman, *Fates* 404, thinks them brave to have resisted, yet is it creditable that they do not stop the slaughter of all the priests and their families?

[17] Peter D. Miscall, *1 Samuel: A Literary Reading* (Bloomington: Indiana University Press, 1986) 134, well observes that Saul continuously misuses the sacred.

ing a king was that he would fight the people's battles, we now see that the men of Israel will be pressed into service to promote Saul's vendetta against his enemy David. As the next several chapters will show, David has only to lie in wait and Saul will come. Saul has accused David of lying in wait for him, a charge that, as before, Saul will make come true. Let us look quickly at two such episodes that initiate the pattern for our next chapter. As Polzin suggests, this section and the whole of chapters 20–23 works off discrepancies in information.[18]

The first episode (23:1-14) pictures David—not Saul—aiming to rescue the people of Keilah from Philistine oppression, a setting reminiscent, perhaps, of the challenge to Saul back in chapter 11. As promised by God, whom David carefully consults, the triumph is David's. Saul hears of it and moves in, hoping to catch David in a trap. Saul, ephodless and priestless, is no match for David with priest and ephod and communication from God. Learning not only that Saul is on his way but that the people of Keilah are willing to betray their recent rescuer, David escapes, and Saul's pursuit is thwarted.[19]

A Jonathan interlude occurs (23:15-18), splitting his father's pursuit. Jonathan, whom the narrator tags here as Saul's son, meets David secretly and reassures him. Jonathan's words about God's plans, like Saul's, miss the mark substantially, stressing the difference in knowledge of the Saulides from David: "Do not be afraid, for the hand of my father Saul shall not find you; you shall be king over Israel, and I shall be second to you; my father Saul also knows that this is so." Jonathan's language speaks not so much of David's survival but of his own: I will be second. Jonathan asserts here that Saul knows that David is destined to rule rather than Jonathan, a point the king will concede soon but has not yet said in our hearing. And they made, the narrator says, a pact before Yʜᴡʜ.

But in the next narrative moment, when Saul is informed by yet another group still loyal to him that David is at Horesh (23:19-29), Saul sets out yet again. Sounding almost excessively grateful that someone has given him information, he blesses them by Yʜᴡʜ for sparing him, though sending them back to double check their information, to learn the neighborhood—after which Saul will come for David: "I am told that he is very cunning," Saul remarks, sounding as though this information as well has reached him second hand. Is his caution a result of the Keilah episode,

---

[18] Polzin, *Samuel and the Deuteronomist* 200–204.

[19] Edelman asks (*Saul* 186) if Keilah is an Israelite city, and what it means that Saul would attack it. David M. Gunn, *The Fate of King Saul: An Interpretation of a Biblical Story* (Sheffield: JSOT Press, 1980) 89 suggests that Saul is acting like a Philistine.

where David slipped Saul's grasp? Is it an effort to test further the quality of his intelligence? But as Saul (searching, pursuing, closing in [v. 25]) draws near, David again learns of it and drops farther south (hurrying to escape Saul and his men, who are closing in and about to capture David [v. 27])—with only a mountain remaining between them. But just as the end looks near (what end is not so clear), a messenger arrives for Saul, telling of a Philistine raid, begging the king's presence. So Saul breaks off pursuit of David, giving a name to the place: Rock of Portions. From there David goes up as well, after Saul, to the strongholds of En-gedi. The scene provides a loophole, but for whom? Do we trust the single messenger who arrives with news of the Philistine raid? Do we, perhaps, sense conspiracy here, knowing that if Jonathan is in some way involved in it the men of Ziph may be as well? Is it too early for Saul and David to meet? Who is controlling the pace of the chase? What is the aim of the chase? Who is the pursuer, who the pursued? It is a dynamic we shall continue to watch and mine as the mad chase intensifies.

CHAPTER SEVEN

Sensing the Silent (1 Samuel 24–26)

"But now that the end of Saul's reign draws near, we begin to see
that false start and providential delay are simply two ways of ex-
pressing the inexpressible mystery of God's dealings with Israel,
and that the abortive reign of Saul is but a prefiguring of that abor-
tion of God's rule which is kingship itself."

Robert Polzin,
Samuel and the Deuteronomist

As I suggested in the last chapter, pursuit is all that remains for Saul
until the evening before his death. We will spend another chapter on it,
concentrating on three things. First, it becomes clearer that David is pursuing Saul rather than the reverse. Second, the weight of the matter changes
from *whether* Saul will find David to *how* the king will die—and how he
must *not* perish. And third, we will see some intense portrayal of why
kingship must perish. As has been our practice, we will focus on the particularities of speech, especially since we have here a rare phenomenon:
face-to-face conversation between Saul and David.[1] We will see intense
(in)capacity for answerability and ponder in several ways the genres that
structure these chapters. After a few general comments I will offer some
assertions about the significance of the similarity between chapters 24 and

---

[1] We have only witnessed speech between them on two occasions: the Goliath battle
(17:32-37, 58) and the Merab proposal (18:17-18). For all of their entanglement, direct encounters have been used very sparingly.

26, then briefly consider each story, and finally turn more major attention to the intervening chapter 25.

Saul is bent on remaining king. God has not moved to dislodge him, David has failed to oust him, Saul's priests have been eliminated, and his prophet Samuel—long silent—is about to die (25:1). Saul's tracking of David continues, as we just saw when Saul followed David to Keilah and Adullam (ch. 23). Saul has been after David, by degrees, since he requisitioned him from Jesse (chs. 16–17), made him son-in-law (ch. 18), ordered him from Michal's house and pursued him to Samuel's home (ch. 19). The king has turned violently against those suspected of assisting David— Michal, Jonathan, Elide priests, Benjamin men (chs. 20–22). To add the column is to see how ingrown has become Saul's sense of his rule, whose single purpose now seems to be to eliminate David. It may appear inevitable that Saul will find David sooner or later, but that is not to be. As we look at the material of the present chapters the advantage is clearly David's and the question for him is a matter of restraint: Saul must die, but David must not kill him. We are—have been all along—dealing not simply with the story of one monarch but of the monarchy. Kingship has become a parody of its "one thing needful" (its role of guarding the YHWH-Israel relationship) and so will perish. How it is to end is not obvious, since our "storyline" Saul survives yet, as for sixth-century readers there remains in exile an anointed of YHWH with heirs, support, and the legitimacy of tradition. Besides the portrait of a struggling human being we are discerning the closing down of an institution, tracing a riddle propounded for a sixth-century audience.

One way to talk about the matter of how the monarch(y) will terminate is to consider a device Bakhtin calls a loophole. I suggested in the last chapter that part of Saul's situation is his inability to imagine a Saul-self that is not king. He so coincides with the role he desires that there is no slippage between it and his self. This utter fit puts him wholly at odds with God, since there is nothing comprising Saul's self-portrait except royalty, on which he and God disagree. A loophole (simply put) is the capacity of one—Saul here, but David and God as well—to slip out of such a finalized, perfectly matched, constricted sense of himself that either he or someone else wants to pronounce. Edges that might constrict can also allow passage through themselves. In the three biblical chapters ahead of us we can watch Saul offered such a loophole, wriggle into it, but lapse back. We will also see David, in danger of killing the king, take great care to avoid both the appearance and fact of regicide. And we must consider God's role in the matter as well. The sameness of the episodes demands that we focus attentively on the dynamic that presses forward so insistently. The three chapters are carefully woven at a number of levels, with resemblances extending far beyond their obvious content.[2] Thrice prominent is the delay hovering around Saul, which has been rehearsed at a number of other places in the story as well, notably in the story of Hannah and her "asked" son. The odd timing of the king's foreshortened and extended rule, his being no sooner hired than fired, is intensely significant in the longer story of Israel and kings.[3]

Before turning brief attention to chapters 24 and 26, which frame chapter 25, let me sum up what I think they together assert. In each framing episode Saul learns of David's whereabouts and goes to seek him with several thousand select men (24:1-2; 26:1-2). But Saul's initial advantage turns quickly to disadvantage as the quarry spots the hunter before the seeker finds the sought (24:3; 26:3-7). While David thus has a visual edge on Saul—sees him without being seen back—there is conversation between David and his men about how to maximize the supposed gift of the moment. In each case a verbal suggestion from David's men—a quotation by them of speech that is new to us, or a distortion of what we have been privy to—urges that David act (or authorize action) against Saul (24:4; 26:8). David, absorbing the suggestion, finally parries it each time (24:6-7; 26:9-11) but not without first performing an action that is symbolically as violent as the suggestion of his men had been (24:4-5; 26:12). Once that action is complete, David engages Saul in conversation about the pursuit of the king (24:8-15; 26:13-16, 18-20, 22-24), putting a rather different slant on his own recent gesture; Saul concedes David's viewpoint (24:16-21; 26:17, 21, 25), bringing each episode to an end (24:22; 26:25). The gain on Saul's previous efforts to track David in chapter 23 can be seen: In these present episodes Saul comes closer to David, but David successfully turns and confronts his pursuer rather than simply escaping as he had done in chapter 23. Though a change in the relative positions of the two is clear enough by the end of each episode, not much will come from the progress. That is, the story's ultimate resolution of the problem of kingship is not very dependent upon the actual outcomes of negotiations held in these chapters—strange though that seems, given the radical nature of Saul's concessions. At one level these encounters serve to run out the clock; at another they reinforce the importance of the chase with its reversal of roles.

[2] See Robert M. Polzin, *Samuel and the Deuteronomist: A Literary Study of the Deuteronomic History: 1 Samuel* (San Francisco: Harper & Row, 1989) 205–12.

[3] Found throughout Polzin's ch. 7, these points are brought together on pp. 212–15.

Saul and David converse: (1 Samuel 24)

We first notice that when Saul is, unaware, in the cave where David is hiding, David's men urge him to something startling: "Here is the day of which the LORD said to you, 'I will give your enemy into your hand, and you shall do to him as it seems good to you'" (24:4). It is a permission we have not heard: not at David's anointing, not when David inquires about Saul's pursuit of him. However, it echoes elements of David's speech at 17:34-37 and 20:16; it is language that Saul struggles boastfully but unsuccessfully to make his own in 23:7. The identification of Saul as David's enemy has been made by the narrator explicitly in 18:29 (after a series of adversarial moves on Saul's part) and implicitly on other occasions when Saul exudes hostility toward David. Though in theory the "missing" words can have been said "offscreen," good storytelling suggests not. We have here a loophole, offered perhaps sincerely to David by his men, a release from the restraint he has heretofore shown. It may be the most popular escape hatch ever, the claim that God validates what we desire to do. The language here redirects us to examine the role of God, who, in our narrative, has seen to the anointing of a pair of kings. This theological language is like oath language: it would implicate God in human schemas, make God a party to our hopes and plans. Here is a blank check from God, David's men urge; fill it in as you wish.

My sense here is that, while loudly denying it, David comes close to succumbing to this escape from restraint. He cuts an edge of Saul's robe, which scholars classify as symbolic castration, assassination, or coup. Though David asserts—immediately to his men and shortly to Saul—that he has kept his hand from harm, that is not so unambiguously clear. David talks of clean hands while holding the royal swatch, shrinks his deed verbally while underlining it visually. He recoils after he has done the snipping but we do not hear precisely why; the narrator simply observes it to us. David's language also makes God complicit, valorizing God for restraining him from raising a hand against God's anointed. That the action might have been worse, as David claims, need not blind us to seeing it as more aggressive than his previous move. David's language to Saul professes innocence, as before, cautioning Saul against those who say David seeks Saul's harm. David asks Saul to witness what was done behind his back, implicitly demanding that we revise what we have seen. David asks the king to read the garment slice as David does—could have been worse —rather than, as might be argued, bad enough. As a gesture, the snipping is subtly violent. It is a dialogical utterance that David formulates from his long relationship with Saul, which Saul has helped shape.

Saul, apparently more credulous than am I, calls his opponent "my son David" and weeps, for what reason he does not specify. Saul's words suggest that he accepts both David's men's theology and David's interpretation of his own action. Saul counterposes a question: "Who has ever found an enemy and yet sent the enemy safely away?"—a question inviting more answers than the "no one" most obviously implied. Like David's language, this word of Saul has a doubled referent. Not only has David let Saul slip away—with only a piece of royal robe sacrificed—but insofar as Saul has been pursuing an enemy (a charge he mostly does not accept, but we may see has some truth to it) he is going to let David go away as well. Each man accepts the loophole offered by his royal opponent and avoids regicide.

The chapter concludes with two more admissions from Saul. First he says, "Now I know that you shall surely be king and that the kingdom of Israel will be established in your hand. . . ." This is an insight we have not heard from Saul up to this point—except in his exclamation of 18:8 where it was plausibly more feared than felt, an early permission for Saul to move against David. Jonathan has indicated that Saul knows, but Jonathan has been shown myopic in regard to his father's inner workings. Jonathan himself has disclosed the same knowledge—starting perhaps with his gift to David at 18:1-5, compounded by his words of commitment to David (20:12-17), and reinforced most recently by his claim that he would be David's second (23:17-18), which will not come to pass. Saul indicates no such expectation here: to the contrary; heirs of Saul and Jonathan become endangered with David on the throne. Second, Saul's concluding plea for the life of his heirs, his name, and his house (echoing Jonathan's of 20:14-17 and 23:17) makes stark the danger he senses for his kin (well borne out as the story winds into 2 Samuel). Can Saul trust the man who has just cut his royal garment secretively not to cut off the Saulide line?

Saul and David converse (1 Samuel 26)

We may compare the two chapters that compose the frame of chapter 25 and see a similar structure. In this twin episode David moves into Saul's space and vulnerability, urged by his men: "God has given your enemy into your hand today. . . ." David's companion Abishai actually uses an expression we heard in Saul's mouth when boasting regarding David in 23:7: "God has given him into my hand, for he has shut himself in. . . ." On that occasion of pursuit it became clear that Saul was wrong on both accounts: YHWH's purposes tended otherwise and David had not shut himself into a tight spot. Loophole language is offered David as before: YHWH intends the very thing you have in mind to do. David now takes not an edge of a garment but the royal spear and water jar, without which Saul cannot survive. Saul's spear bespeaks both royal power and impotence; the water jar is the king's life in the wilderness. Abishai's next words also borrow from Saul's character zone, as David's man boasts that *he* (unlike Saul) will not need two thrusts to get *his* man.[4]

David's language shows how much closer he has come to the topic of the king's death: ruminating, rare for him, David ponders the likely circumstances of Saul's death, showing it to be on his mind even as he distances himself from it. David says, "As the LORD lives, the LORD will strike him down; or his day will come to die; or he will go down to battle and perish [literally, be swept away]. The LORD forbid that I should raise my hand. . . ."[5] That David anticipates Saul's death seems clear; he envisions three possible modes of it. That he wants to stay clear of agency is also obvious. The options for kingly demise are interesting: God may strike Saul, though how David imagines that to look is not so clear as it will soon be; it is here primarily a matter of responsibility, since David contrasts all three of these modes with a deed by his own hand. Or Saul's day may come naturally in the course of things. Or he may go down to battle and be swept away, which is what will almost happen—and "the enemy" will be responsible, specifically the convenient Philistines.[6] David's reflection ends in his announcement that whatever the case may be, *he* will not be the agent of Saul's death. The sixth-century subtext is clear: God will take care of the monarch(y), or it will just wither naturally, or an enemy will destroy it. So although these chapters are often seen primarily in terms of what David fears from Saul, prominent as well is what David seems to fear he will do: raise a hand against the king for harm. David has not put forth his hand to his opponent's death yet, but he breaks off as if talking to himself: ". . . take the spear . . . and the water jar, and let us go." No self-recriminations this time, no moral kickback here, and a very different tone as we next listen in on his shouted conversation with the camp of the king.

[4] A simple assertion like 26:8 reminds us how much of the discourse is aimed at ourselves since we, rather than Abishai, know of Saul's pairs of efforts to spear David.

[5] David M. Gunn, *The Fate of King Saul: An Interpretation of a Biblical Story* (Sheffield: JSOT Press, 1980) 103 sees the effect of these words over the sleeping king as a sort of spell, given Saul's ultimate fate.

[6] Swept away is the fate with which Samuel closes his address to the people of Israel in ch. 12 if they do evil, a fate to be shared by them and their king. It is one of the ways in which the narrator may intend, but the reader may surely construe that Saul stands for something larger than himself, kingship in general (Polzin, *Samuel and the Deuteronomist* 213–15). The monarchic mode of relationship between God and people would be my way of saying it.

David first speaks of the king to Saul's man Abner, charging *him* with disarming and endangering the king. David's language places the onus on the man who did not prevent such a breach and on the near-victim, leaving little room to accuse the one who engineered the deed. David verbally directs the attention of Saul's camp to the missing spear and water jar. To risk the life by failing to guard the anointed of YHWH is a capital offense, David says, with the ambiguity of reference he always manages by not naming the king. We can, I think, hear another doubled address of the words, aimed at Abner but past him at Saul; if we think ahead we can hear a triple relevance. It is a clever opener. As before, David utilizes what his men said, standing behind them and pointing to their language to make it enhance his own restraint. As perhaps intended and in any case now provoked, the reply comes not from Abner but from Saul, who asks once again (as in 24:16), "Is that your voice, my son David?"

David replies formally, "It is my voice, my lord, O king,"[7] moving without prostration to his now familiar—and clearly central—question: "What guilt is on my hands?" Giving Saul no chance to answer (and disregarding or failing to acknowledge the two items his hand has just removed from the sleeping king), David proposes two of the various possibilities: "If it is the LORD who has stirred you up against me, may he accept an offering; but if it is mortals, may they be accursed before the LORD for they have driven me out today from my share of the heritage of the LORD. . . ." The third possibility, that David himself bears responsibility for the situation, is not articulated directly. Insofar as David is laying a trace for Saul and then tracking him along it as well, he confuses that trail by accusing Saul of tracking *him;* and not only in the deed but in language, not quite bloodily but surely symbolically, David turns against Saul the weapons the king would wield against David. David, as before (24:14), draws himself as small quarry, a lone partridge, a single flea, hounded by a mighty royal.[8] David makes himself the endangered one—which we may read over against the fact that we have never seen Saul close in on David very proximately. I am not saying that the king is not powerful or that we have not heard and seen him lethal in his pursuit of David; but I am

---

[7] Peter D. Miscall, *1 Samuel: A Literary Reading* (Bloomington: Indiana University Press, 1986) 161 hears scorn intoned by David here; cf. Jan P. Fokkelman, *Narrative Art and Poetry in the Books of Samuel: Volume II: The Crossing Fates* (Assen, The Netherlands: Van Gorcum, 1986) 467, who thinks Saul now confronts the real David instead of his own fantasy of him.

[8] The issue David raises about his opponent inciting him to idolatry is not so clear and must, unfortunately, be omitted from discussion, important though it no doubt is.

remembering and reminding that we have never seen David "winged" by Saul. David is always (to reintonate his own language from 20:3 and 27:1) a step ahead. Part of David's pursuit is to make Saul look like the aggressor. It is not a wholly false move, but it leaves Saul bearing more of the blame than is quite accurate to the saga we have seen. It misleads us slightly as we look back at the king. David's rhetoric is convincing, if we can judge by a sampling of commentators. Whether this is a conscious strategy on David's part is also not clear, but it need not be malevolent. It is part of David's need to escape from Saul and to counter Saul's refusal to cede the rule to David. David, we must recall, has only heard once from Jonathan and once from Saul that the old king understands that David is to succeed him. Part of what activates David into whatever strategy we may discern for him is his resistance to Saul's refusal to quit his post.

But whatever the case, Saul accedes to what David has said, backing away from harm to David as we have seen him do several times (18:21; 19:7; 20:26; 23:28; 24:20) amid the many moments where he lunges after him in one way or another. Saul's resistance to David's power is strongest when David is not in his presence; faced with David, Saul tends to bend toward him. "I have done wrong; come back, my son David, for I will not harm you again because my life was precious in your sight today; I have been a fool . . ."[9] (also similar to 24:17-19). David has not claimed responsibility for the spear and the water jar, though Saul seems to assume that David again has had Saul in his sight(s) and then let him go unharmed. Polzin sees the two gestures of cutting the robe and taking the water and weapon as a perfect rejoinder to Saul's treatment of David, well designed to bring Saul to contrition; various others see them as gentle deeds.[10] I think they are powerful, double-voiced assaults on Saul's person/position, not gracious in any real sense at all. A hint of violence may be threat enough, but what Saul does not suggest—on either occasion—is that David's "sparing" (cutting the garment edge and removing the spear and water) approaches very near to harming the king. That is, Saul accepts, makes persuasive to himself, David's words on the matter of their relationship. But amid the language setting Saul up as a threat against David—language Saul is now eager for both to escape—I sense the opposite: David is far more dangerous to Saul than Saul to David. How will David escape his own strength and temptation in this matter?

Only after Saul has spoken words to which David makes no direct reply does David tell Abner to send someone to retrieve the king's items.

---

[9] Saul accepts here the exact accusation Samuel had made in 13:13.
[10] Polzin, *Samuel and the Deuteronomist* 207.

Though we know David has been in Saul's camp, this information cannot be welcome to the Saulides. David concludes with a speech about justice and fidelity, oddly impersonal, with specific referents obscured except in terms of the case he has been sketching, concluding with the construction of his men: YHWH permitted it but I forbore. David concludes by blessing himself on the basis of his restraint: As he, David, guarded the king's life today, so may YHWH guard David's life and spare him from tribulation. David does not, now, ask mercy from Saul but from God, puts himself under debt to the deity, not to the king. And Saul, in what are his final words to David, blesses his general undertakings—an odd sort of "have a nice day" comment.[11] Here are mutual loopholes once again, as these two break off their last tussle and retreat to their corners, leaving us to ponder the dynamics of regicide. Has David spoken well of God? Has Saul intuited something about God as well? This is a good moment to ponder your sense of the deity in this long story.

Dreaming of Saul enacted (1 Samuel 25)

The basic similarity of this interlude to the royal chase we have just witnessed is not difficult to see. Let me review the factors that rekey the present chapter to the other two under discussion here. The "David" character learns the whereabouts of his lord and sends to negotiate with him (25:2-9); an initial relatedness turns sour as the petitioned superior repudiates the message of the petitioner with its implications of entitlement (25:10-11). Outside the knowledge of the superior, conversation between the upstart and his men brings their adversary into danger, with an aggression undisguised but not perceived by its object until quite late (25:12 and forward). But what enters new here is a mediating figure, a voice of counsel and restraint to the David, acting against the ostensible interests of the powerful incumbent character, purportedly for the good of his household and lineage, all threatened (by gestures and words in 25:21-22, 33-34). Negotiation occurs (25:24-31), with the result that violence is intercepted, repudiated, but also made redundant since someone from the household hands over the goods under contention—or at least a down payment on them—with the suggestion that more may come later (v. 31, picked up in 25:39-42). The character whose goods are plundered by his own intimate has a "heart episode" when he learns of it, which he does shortly after his

---

[11] David Jobling, *1 Samuel* (Collegeville: The Liturgical Press, 1998) 92, is one of few who does not see insincerity in Saul but indecision; Saul does not really know what he wants as regards David.

celebrating his achievements; he dies a bit later, and then more of his goods pass into the hands of the erstwhile subaltern (25:36-38). This whole scene, which I suggest we see as a sort of (day)dream, is fragmentary and incomplete as that genre typically is, leaving wholly outside our confident decision the question of which man is right and which wrong; the Abigail is a similarly ambivalent figure.[12] So though the plot of 24/26 reruns, the voice of restraint—the loophole the David character needs—moves outside his own throat and is taken up by another character, while the need for such discipline is obviated by the death of the opponent.

On what bases rests the genre case that will allow us to construe this episode as a dream of David's lethal pursuit of Saul where the actual death comes off, though without David's hands being bloodied? We have a narrative of how the king(ship) will die, woven tightly with insistence on how it must not. My case for a dream genre rests on four factors. First, a rough analogy is established between Nabal and Saul: shared geographic locations of Carmel and Maon (15:12; 23:24); common shepherding task; characterization of both as externally powerful but simultaneously vulnerable; a *"nomen est omen"* quality, since Nabal's name signifies "fool" (25:3, 25) as Saul's has been shown to mean "ask." The tangled relation between the Nabal and the David resembles closely the one we have been tracking, where the "inferior," whether invited or asserting himself or some blend of both, makes a claim of entitlement that contests their power equation. The shared discourse is flavored with father/son terminology, with the elder abusive and the younger at least superficially deferential. When the Nabal attempts simply to "just say no," the David goes for the jugular of the whole household, risking whatever bound their two enterprises. In contrast to the more carefully parsed actions of chapters 24 and 26, this David acts without modulation of aggression.

Second for my case is the presence throughout our long Saul narrative of selftalk that rehearses deadly plans somewhat candidly; the genre daydream or fantasy is at one level simply a great elaboration of such announcements to "ourselves." This narrative segment catches at the roughest and least tamed edges of both Saul and David: the Nabal is Saul at his most churlish and isolated, having asked for what comes to him; the David here is violent until stopped and then goes self-congratulatory once he has

---

[12] Abigail is often (nowadays) valorized as a strong feminine character; she may as easily be vilified for her breach of a set of culture patterns and, of course, for the death of her husband. Feminist analysis is not easy here, and in my opinion there should be some hesitation about ripping the story out of context and using it as an abstract example. A thorough feminist critique would, I think, make a complex and nonstereotypical case for this character.

gained what he wants without having to compromise his position. These two portraits are worst-self scenarios, distorted but recognizable. The third base for my genre choice is the strangely intrusive (and underdeveloped) deep sleep that has visited Saul's camp, lingering on some characters as chapter 26 opens, encouraging me to bring it forward from this present chapter. That is, the story has heretofore been filled with detail that defies realism, e.g., David's approaching Saul closely enough to slice his robe while the king is otherwise occupied. There is no need to resort to a special sleep from God except that it signal in some additional way. Fourth, a notice of the death of Samuel (which will become relevant at chapter 28 and be repeated again there) cuts off the two kings from his advice and jolts the narrative out of his control as well. That is, the removal of Samuel intensifies the likelihood that these two prophet-anointeds must resolve their problem themselves. This episode is a "dreaming of Saul," floating narratively between the characters (and us), which, in the manner of dreams, brings factors of their experience into strange relation. Borrowing a term, I will call this episode a sideshadow, a brief foray into a genre of fantasy in which the David character contemplates more directly the manner of changing the royal guard but in a way that does not actually happen in the story we have. Since in fact the death of the dynastic father has already occurred symbolically and is about to occur in the story line just ahead, this scene backshadows as well. As the riddle genre is making present here a problem of sixth-century leadership, it foreshadows.[13]

What is different here from the scenes that frame this present episode is the intervention of an other—the Abigail—to the David character. In chapters 24 and 26 David, in twisting the rationale urged on him by his men (God wills you to slay the king), provided a loophole for Saul, simultaneously shaping one for himself. That is, though his men urged him to take advantage of his opponent, and though David was arguably tempted and to some extent convinced, he restrained himself from excess and in each case let Saul go, talking the matter out against the urgings of his men and then repositioning his utterances favorably to himself. Saul contributed to their loopholes by his own demeanor, showing himself little threat to David. Each loosens his grip on the other and simultaneously frees himself from a crime. But here we have quite another elaboration. The Abigail character, playing the role given earlier to Jonathan (e.g., ch. 20), constructs David's escape route more blatantly. As is well described in the

---

[13] The term is coined and developed (with some clear differences) by Bakhtin scholar Gary Saul Morson, *Narrative Freedom and the Shadows of Time* (New Haven: Yale University Press, 1994) 20–42.

chapter, she interposes herself between the David and the revenge upon which he is bent, acts to stopgap the violence not only by her talk of justice but by taking the goods of the Nabal and giving them to David (a move he completes when he marries her [vv. 39-42, but read the chapter's last two verses while you are on site!]). Her words to the David (25:26-31) clarify all he has to lose by moving violently, perhaps unjustly against a whole household and draw in beautiful language the care with which she maintains that YHWH has guarded the David from doing this very thing and has stored good things for a righteous man. But she also gains for him all his objectives by another route. David's words of rejoinder (25:32-35) reinforce her point of view, though suggesting that he sees her as a petitioner as well as—instead of—a benefactor. This flipflop, unexpected in the circumstances, helps certify David's kingly role.[14] The Abigail shows not only how but why the monarchy will perish: David claims the estate of a man who expired from learning how he had been thwarted.

The problem that becomes acute now, which may have been troubling you for some time in this story, is the role in which all seem to cast God. In case you are not yet worried about it, let us visit the fantasy's ending (vv. 36-38). The Abigail, having moved in a way most shocking (in terms of the likely cultural constraints), disrespects her husband and ensures that he loses honor not only before his enemy but in his own household.[15] Then, having already plundered his goods with the help of his servants and turned them over to his enemy, she returns to find her husband at his last meal—a fine one—clearly oblivious of threat. Refraining from speech until the next day, she then speaks words that stun the Nabal into incapacity, his heart becoming like a great stone. Ten days later, our narrator says, "the LORD struck Nabal and he died" (25:38). So the loopholes through which Saul and David have been slipping shift now, freeing "David" to be both just and king, tightening on "Saul" so that he dies, implicating "God" in a way perhaps more deadly than is the case for the monarchy. Our last task here is to comment briefly on God's role in the death of the king.

As we recall, the manner in which a king was asked was distressing to God, insofar as it disregarded divine input, experience, and opinion. Worse,

---

[14] Jobling, *1 Samuel* 155, is one who notes that David's response in some ways ill suits the immediate context. That is, David seems to be responding to something else, comes to deal with Abigail as though she were a "simple" petitioner. Miscall, *1 Samuel* 153, characterizes David's speech as pompous and self-focused. I am tempted to see it as a gender issue.

[15] Consult for these points Philip Esler, "The Madness of Saul: A Cultural Reading of 1 Samuel 8-31," in J. Cheryl Exum and Stephen D. Moore, eds., *Biblical Studies/Cultural Studies* (Sheffield: Sheffield Academic Press, 1998).

the community's ignoring of God while seeking a king made painfully prominent the decayed nature of their relationship, at least from the human point of view. It was this deficiency that God mourned while acceding to the demand. And God's words, as has been suggested several times, stress that the relationship between God and people is what matters most to God and must concern the king as well. Saul, in retrospect, was not a good choice for the job, which means—in our double lens of seeing him as both an individual and an institution—that "he" cannot do the job of "minding," in the fullest sense of that word, the ancient-and-current bonds that clasp together God and people. The inability is made clear by the total lack of communication between God and "Saul"—man and monarch—and by Saul's deteriorating capacity to relate to anyone else as well, himself included. His kingship, which he has steadfastly refused to vacate even after he knows it is no longer legitimate, will go deadly now in every aspect. So the narrative has closed in on the manner of death. Saul seems unlikely to resign; David must not kill him. Though the enemy will provide the proximate occasion of death, in our fantasy—as well as in its surrounding discourse of 24:4, 10, 12, and 15, and 26:8-11—God is here named agent in the Nabal dream. Is this the portrait of God that we must hang on our wall?

We have, here and elsewhere in the Bible (and perhaps closer still to home) humans struggling to make sense of experience that they—we—assume in one way or another includes God. Such project is crucial, both in our "nonbiblical lives" and while we interpret Scripture. The three chapters we are working with contain some twenty-five assertions about God's will. Our caution must be about accepting in a facile way what we want to be true. Though David's men urge one picture of God handing Saul over to David, David both denies and expands it. He picks it up, revises it, and then offers it as his own, both nudging his opponent and looking generous. The narrator of our story, who has been rather careful in the lineaments of God's portrait, floats this fantastic scene where the death of "the man"—though credited bluntly to God—is in fact shared out in the story's detail, naming as complicit the Nabal himself, the David, the Abigail, even the servants, with God's role pasted on only at the moment of the last heartbeat. The whole manner of recital undercuts a flat assertion that God kills "the king," sending us back, appropriately, to refigure the problem. The careful discourse, the weighting of answerability, and the genre of fantasy or dream construct God's loophole here—or ours. That the Nabal, refusing relation with all, has become an utter isolate, eating his last meal heedless of the calamity that is galloping toward his heritage, belies the simplistic—and hence provocative—assertion that God killed the Nabal. Biblical portraits of God, because they are multiple and usually done with great care, demand equal care from us. Our experience is always inevitably our starting point—granted that, like the figure whose heart turns to stone, we must be answerable to some extent for the kind of experience we have. Idolatry is the besetting sin in the Hebrew Bible: false reification of God, whether in material or in word.

As we bring these three chapters to a close, having seen what, how, and why the king will go down, the one thing remaining in Saul's story is to watch his death. It should not startle us to learn that David is far from the scene when it happens. How the other players are positioned, and what becomes the choice of Saul himself, may surprise us.

CHAPTER EIGHT

Final Questions (1 Samuel 27–2 Samuel 1)

> "To read chapter 31 is to reread previous texts, indeed all of 1 Samuel and beyond, with new information and from new perspectives."
>
> Peter Miscall, *1 Samuel*

How do *you* think the king will die, given your reading so far? As you reflect briefly on that final question before we consider it together, keep in mind the double referent of the character Saul: both a fragile human being and an epitome for Israel's extensive experience with monarchy. How to bring such a project—such projects—to an end? The scenes we have just watched all underline the negative edge: for one of YHWH's people to lift a hand against YHWH's anointed cannot be justified. The end must come in some other way. Another momentum becomes increasingly obvious here: David's prominence in the narrative intensifies just as Saul's wanes. Our storyteller accomplishes, orchestrates a *ritard* and a *fortissimo* simultaneously, signaling differently with different parts of the storyline. Another way to put that same point is to say that the narrator is on the verge of proceeding with the traditional story of Davidic kings that culminates late in the sixth century while signaling simultaneously that the institution David's heirs construct is already moribund, appearances to the contrary notwithstanding. The question to be deliberated by the sixth-century audience is how to terminate kingship appropriately.

Of the six chapters here, three are devoted to getting David away from the vicinity of Saul's battle (27, 29–30). We will not follow the David story into 2 Samuel and Kings, so it must suffice here to stipulate that the main insistence, articulated in many times and ways, is that David is nowhere near the neighborhood when Saul dies on Mount Gilboa.[1] The three chapters focusing on Saul include his visit to the medium of En-dor on the eve of battle (ch. 28), his death and that of his sons on Gilboa (ch. 31), and finally the significance of the multiple responses to his death when it is received in various quarters (1 Samuel 31 and 2 Samuel 1).[2] Polzin summarizes the tendency of many elements of these last chapters to bring us back to the "parables" of chapters 1–3 and 4–6: false starts and providential delays, night visions, foretellings of death of dynastic heirs, Philistine foes, destructive guests, and the falling of the high are all reused from 1 Samuel 27 to 2 Samuel 1.[3] The matters of genre, discourse, and answerability that have propelled us thus far will carry us again.

Saul is prepared for death (1 Samuel 28)

This visual scene, a favorite with artists, offers the king a mirror in which to glimpse something important if he is able; we, standing behind him, watch from a slightly different angle. Saul is shown his monarchic self about to collapse. We need to watch over Saul's shoulder the isolated man but also the whole royal experience presented microcosmically. We may bring to the mirror other desires as well, perhaps the lineaments of a human being who feels utterly abandoned and deeply fearful. The urgency of Philistine massing prompts Saul a final time. Israel's king has been distracted from Israel's foe as Saul has engaged his opponent, but now he musters his men at Gilboa. At the sight of the Philistines "[Saul] was afraid and his heart trembled greatly" (28:5). And Saul asks, inquires of YHWH by dreams, by lots, by prophets. But YHWH, who has never yet spoken directly to Saul in our story, does not answer now by any of these means. Saul's asking, as perennially, is inadequate and ineffective. Though he asks, we also recognize his own complicity in the silence evoked, for Saul has misused God's spirit, has driven away the priestly lots-bearer, has disregarded his prophet's words. And we learn that, as Saul had eliminated the legitimate priestly presence when he slaughtered all but one of the Elide line, he

[1] Robert M. Polzin, *Samuel and the Deuteronomist: A Literary Study of the Deuteronomic History: 1 Samuel* (San Francisco: Harper & Row, 1989) 216–17.

[2] Though it may appear that the story is split apart already, Jan P. Fokkelman, *Narrative Art and Poetry in the Books of Samuel: Volume II: The Crossing Fates* (Assen, The Netherlands: Van Gorcum, 1986) 555–57, 569, 579 makes an intricate case for ways in which both character discourse and also the shared chronology force the careful reader to keep braiding the "David" and "Saul" episodes together.

[3] Polzin, *Samuel and the Deuteronomist* 217–21.

has also driven the less legitimate intermediaries from his land.[4] But, like Abiathar who survived Saul's violence, apparently one medium remains. And so Saul orders his men to seek for him an intermediary to consult. And his men assure him that there is a woman at En-dor, not so far from Gilboa. The stress here is not so much on the illegality of the means Saul must use to gain access to Samuel but on his desperate asking, his being reduced to beseeching the outlawed and the dead for advice. Both Saul's egregious violation of his basic charge to mind the YHWH-Israel bond and his more pedestrian ineffectual leadership are demonstrated as he violates his own law and makes evident that others have done so as well, including his own men, who seemed well informed about the woman.

Pointlessly, needlessly, even poignantly, Saul disguises himself and steals off by night for this inquiry. From whom is Saul disguising himself? Commentators speculate that he hides from Philistines, from his own fighting men, from the woman herself; one scholar parses the particular Hebrew word here to draw from it the sense that Saul's disguise makes himself absent—hence sought for.[5] It is not the familiar word for "ask" that constructs Saul's name so overtly, but it is a synonym of sorts, insofar as a disguise invites readers, at least, to ask again about Saul's identity. What strikes me is that he adopts the guise of a "not king," the very role to which God has been persuading him presumably, though it has registered with Saul as silence. It is surely the role Samuel urged upon him at the end of the Amalekite episode (ch. 15) and will mandate again shortly. For whom is that a disguise? Most notably, himself. Saul here takes—if unreflectively—the role he has been resisting so assiduously and goes to listen to his old prophet. Saul's disguise is actually his nonroyal self, most likely to hear what he needs to learn. In Bakhtin's loophole language, Saul's disguise provides the non-coincidence between himself and his royal identity that may furnish him an escape.

When Saul and his two companions arrive at their destination the king engages with the woman in five quick exchanges (28:8-14). Saul's first approach is guarded, testing her willingness and ability to bring up anyone before specifying whom he wants to contact. She rejoins defensively and carefully: Saul has cut off all mediums from the land, and to ask her to do the forbidden thing is to snare her and risk her life. She does not say she cannot do it, but that it is dangerous for her to do it, associating with the venture heavy words: cut off, snare, death. Countering her concern, Saul promises her safety on oath by YHWH. But are Saul's oaths reliable? Can

---

[4] Deut 18:9-26.
[5] Richard Coggins, "On Kings and Disguises," *JSOT* 50 (1991) 56.

Yhwh be made partner to this particular oath? Apparently convinced, however we may feel, she asks him for further direction. "Bring up Samuel for me," her visitor specifies. The medium's reaction comes not when she hears the name but when she sees Samuel. Though she knows the identity of the one she is summoning, the sight of him, called up, exposes the identity of the royal asker.[6] Accusing her customer of deceiving her, she cries, "You are Saul!"

Before going ahead with Saul's reaction let us rehearse some of the possibilities exposed in the contending discourse of these two. Most obviously (in Hebrew), the medium's choice of verb for "deceive" constructs a pun on the word for the garments Saul wears as disguise. Though in context her accusation about the deception seems clearly linked with her fears of being entrapped to do what the king has made illegal, this story's love of wordplay cautions us against reducing her words to a single meaning. Her accusation also reintonates Saul's words to his soldiers at 14:33: "You have dealt treacherously [with me]. . . ." We may also sense a deeper reference to the monarchy's cardinal sin: purporting to sustain while depleting the relations with God. But the more intriguing question may be why her seeing the prophet helps her identify the king. How does the prophet's presence give away the king's identity? How do the powers the woman taps help her see more deeply past disguises into identities? The utterance itself may be key, since the woman's Hebrew expression, "You are *sha'ul*," makes a frame of sorts with Hannah's "He is *sha'ul*" (2:28). That she sees Samuel but identifies Saul takes us back to the implied equivalence of Samuel and "the Saul" in chapters 1–3, but to what end? The medium's words call our attention a final time to the necessary partnership between king and prophet that has gone so awry; we see its importance a final time in its failure. But whatever the richness of layers of signification, Saul reassures her again, pressing her about what she sees, directing us to that as well. As several have observed, the woman seems to see and Saul to hear; whether he can see the apparition of the prophet is not indicated, nor is it evident that the medium hears their conversation.[7] She describes first a divine being coming up out of the ground, and when prompted for more detail she describes an old man, wrapped in a robe. That specification evidently assures Saul that it is Samuel that she sees. And he prostrates before the presence of the dead prophet. Is such a gesture appropriate, this falling of the king before a shade?

[6] See Pamela Tamarkin Reis, "Eating the Blood: Saul and the Witch of En-dor," *JSOT* 73 (1997) 11–12.

[7] W.A.M. Beuken, "I Samuel 28: The Prophet as 'Hammer of Witches,'" *JSOT* 6 (1978) 7.

Next comes the conversation between prophet and king, apparently the heart of the chapter. The narrator draws back here and the characters discuss old matters directly, by an exchange of questions.[8] "Why have you disturbed me, bringing me up?" the prophet asks. Though commentary tends to focus on the implications of what "disturbing" implies about Israelite views on afterlife, I think the weight of the question is on "what do you want? why am I here?" And indeed it is to this level of the query that Saul answers: "I am in great distress, for the Philistines are warring against me, and God has turned away from me and answers me no more, either by prophets or dreams; so I have summoned you to tell me what I should do." It is a moment of great intensity in this long narrative, perhaps Saul's most exposed moment. His verbs for "distress" and "has turned," paronomasially related in Hebrew, connect to 13:6, where the narrator described Saul's distress at Samuel's failure to appear to help with sacrifices, and to 15:26 and 28, where God and Samuel's turnings away from Saul's kingship become definitive after the Amalekite debacle.[9] That the Philistines are against him is not the heart of his distress; that they may be massing in huger numbers only brings to a head what seems to be Saul's focal anguish: He is cut off in every aspect from guidance—this asker of others; he gets no answer from God through any channels. Saul sounds as if he has at last registered the implications of what has been the case since he resisted the prophet's words in the midst of earlier Philistine battles and at the end of the Amalekite slaughter: Since that refusal to hear, God has rejected Saul's kingship, and the king's disengagement with that firing has put him at odds with God. Saul's continuing to reign has been a husk only. Finally Saul totals the cost of his opposition: great distress at his utter non-relationality with God. As has been obvious, the only information that has reached Saul has come tortuously, wrung from those he suspects of conspiracy: his obfuscating prophet, his son, his daughter, his household, his priests, informers from the desert, and of course David himself. Hence Saul's conclusion: only a dead prophet, his prophet, dead, can breach the gap and tell him what he needs to do. About what? we may wish Samuel had asked him. What is Saul going to do about the silence of God? Who can advise the king on the radical failure of his prime charge of caring for the bond between deity and people?

Samuel's words cover precisely this same old ground, as though since the day they last spoke there is nothing left to say, nothing past that moment relevant to articulate. "Why then do you ask me, since the LORD has

---

[8] Fokkelman charts the exchanges: *Fates* 601.

[9] Diana V. Edelman, *King Saul in the Historiography of Judah* (Sheffield: Sheffield Academic Press, 1991) 246–47.

turned from you and become your enemy?" But in fact I think two new implications arise from this exchange, though their weight may differ for Saul
and for us. For Samuel goes on to say in plain terms something we have not
heard addressed to Saul before: not only has the kingdom been torn from
Saul's hand but "the LORD . . . has given it to your friend David" (28:17,
author's translation). Does Samuel's naming of David force instantaneous
reappraisal of and fresh insight into all that Saul has bent his energies to do
in recent episodes? Rationally, no—since we have seen Saul suspect in his
own selftalk that David is his successor and have heard him concede it first
to Jonathan and finally to David himself. But to learn that YHWH has been
backing David and that Saul's opponent in this matter has been God would
cast it into a new light. Nor, we may note, has Samuel told him what to do.
To say what will happen is not the same as saying how the king is to meet
it. And, as Saul has already been told at some length by Samuel and now
hears reiterated, the root cause remains Saul's disobedience in the matter
of Amalek. Even when confronted relentlessly at the time, Saul still avoided
his charge, so that the killing of King Agag was left to Samuel. That moment is pivotal for everything that has happened.[10] As Saul has dug in, his
purposes have moved resolutely against those of God, who has become an
opponent. Since that moment, described in chapter 15, we have seen other
slaughters by Saul and by David. Though it is tempting to try to organize
this thicket—to line up what is legitimate and what is not in terms of slaying foes—I think the Amalekite matter is of its own type and that Saul's
refusal to complete that task as ordered by God through the prophet is not
explainable by analogy. That is, Saul was fired from being king because of
his refusal to extirpate the ancient foe. That David is simultaneously and
somewhat more successfully coping with Amalekites (chs. 27, 30) makes
Saul's failure and its consequences the more apparent.[11]

Though it is distressing—even scandalous—to certain modern sensi-
bilities to so construct the whole issue of obedience to God on such a matter as genocide, the Deuteronomistic Historian seems clear about it. As we
may recall from the opening words of God in that scene, the "settling" of

---

[10] Beuken, "I Samuel 28," 5, thinks that Samuel refuses consultation; that does not seem
entirely true since he does not refuse to engage. That he says nothing new is not even quite the
case: naming David is new and perhaps useful to Saul. Kenneth M. Craig, Jr., "Rhetorical
Aspects of Questions Answered with Silence in 1 Samuel 14:37 and 28:6," *CBQ* 56 (1994)
234 points out Saul's "amnesia" moments: 13:13-14; 22:18; 23:6, 8-12. Given the resistance
of Saul to hearing the information he nonetheless has been given several times, amnesia is
not the correct word. Reis, "Eating the Blood," 11 adds that the exchange gives Saul new information about the time of his death and the catastrophes for his people that go along with it.

[11] At 30:17 even David lets four hundred escape.

the ancient foe who had harassed YHWH's people during their desert wandering is a score God promised to even once the people were at rest (1 Sam 15:2 and Deut 25:17-19). Saul's refusal to accept this charge is clearly cardinal—and ramified through many alibis and pretendings, as we recall from the discussion between prophet and king. That context was also linked to worship, with Saul claiming that his intent was to offer the best of the Amalekite persons and property to God, and Samuel denounced that gesture as well. The point is not so much who literally were Amalekites but whom they represent in the story of kings. Amalek is every lethal foe with whom the king refuses to deal definitively as charged, to the detriment of the community, at whose flank is massed an ever-stronger enemy. Miscall summarizes: "Samuel condenses the entire narrative of 1 Samuel 16–27 and even chapter 28 into the fulfillment of his denunciation in 1 Sam. 13:13-14 and 1 Sam. 15:22-29."[12] Saul's refusal to obey, compounded by his resistance to acknowledge fully his disobedience, makes him unfit for ruling. That many disobedient kings will follow him does not excuse him, in fact underlines the equation between Saul and monarchy. Saul *is* the monarchic refusal to heed the words the prophet delivers from God about fundamentals. Samuel's final words ring those of the man of God in 2:34 and made visible in chapter 4: the father and his sons will die on the same day and the army be given into the hands of the Philistines. At these words of prophet to king, Saul again falls prostrate, the narrator clarifying that the words of Samuel have not diminished Saul's fear.

Samuel's words have toppled the king. But the narrator clarifies that Saul's lack of physical resources was a factor too; he had been fasting. Why he had fasted seems not the point, though scholars speculate upon it. It seems rather that we are redirected back to the fasting and sonless Hannah, her prayer about the collapse of the mighty, the falling of the heavy Eli that begins to give deeper meaning to her words. In any case, twice here Saul has rehearsed for his ultimate falling, which is to come soon on Mount Gilboa; he helps us to anticipate the collapse of the long monarchic experiment of Israel. The last small event at En-dor seems anti-climactic to some but strikes me as of key importance.[13] When the medium

---

[12] Peter D. Miscall, *1 Samuel: A Literary Reading* (Bloomington: Indiana University Press, 1986) 169.

[13] Reis, who thinks the witch has cast a spell over biblical commentators, reviews what the results of this scholarship have been ("Eating the Blood," 3–4). Reis's argument is that the woman acts, and competently, from motives of self-preservation rather than kindness. She supposes that the shared meal is a mantic sacrifice to the dead that illegally but effectively binds herself and the king and drives Saul to suicide. I cannot follow her conclusions but appreciate her fresh and more critical look at the story dynamics.

sees Saul's fall and his terror, she bargains with him. Insisting on a *quid pro quo,* she says: I risked my life to heed you; now you must . . . heed me. She obeyed; he must obey. Does her logic imply that Saul also risks his life to be fed by the woman? At the level of plot this simple act of hospitality of a proscribed woman to her authoritative king is arguably the kindest gesture we have seen extended to Saul. But it directs us as well to the very end of 2 Kings, where the last surviving king, Jehoiachin—a twin of Saul in some senses—emerges from prison, changes his clothes, and eats at his captor's table. Having paid a price in long captivity, he gets a release though not a restoration. Here the medium insists, overriding Saul's first demur, which so typically for him cannot withstand another's determination of purpose. She slaughters a fatted calf and bakes unleavened bread for the man, who has arisen from the floor to sit on her bed. This intermediary with the realms of the divine resembles a wisdom figure who has prepared a meal for those who need to listen to her (Prov 9:1-6). To feed and strengthen the king is her contribution, perhaps a wasted gesture on the eve of his death. But she has strengthened him to do what he must face, perhaps finally to make some decision for himself. No alibi, no pretending: no one can tell him what he needs to do; were any to do so, there is no guarantee the advice would be right when the moment came. So wisdom's strength is the best gift the king can be given. Having eaten wisdom's meal, Saul and his servants melt away into the night.

How the king dies (1 Samuel 31:1-7)

When the moment finally comes the narrative moves directly to its point. Saul, alone, is once again the focus of the reporting. When the Philistines press, many Israelites fall slain on Gilboa, and the rest flee. The sons of Saul are slain by the Philistines: Jonathan, Abinadab, Malchisua. Saul survives still, fighting on until he is found and wounded by Philistine archers. Saul speaks up for the last time, to a young man who attends him, circling us back to the scene of Saul's first words when he urged his young companion that they should abandon their quest and return home (9:5). "Draw your sword and thrust me through with it, so that these uncircumcised may not come and thrust me through, and make sport of me," the king asks. His words suggest to me not so much fear as desire to die in a manner not undignified. It is his final asking, a last request that someone else resolve his life for him. But, so typically, his request is met with a refusal. The armor-bearer, as we have already heard stressed in chapters 24–26, likely knows better than—fears and refuses—to raise a hand against Yhwh's anointed. Do it for me, Saul asks, but the boy cannot obey. And so

Saul, answerable at last, takes his sword into his own hand and falls upon it, falls slain by his own decision on Mount Gilboa, falls among those who lie there: his sons, now his armor-bearer, and the dead of Israel.

How does Saul fall, how falls the monarchy he embodies? The views of commentators vary, extending from the sense that he is a martyred hero dying honorably to a reading that his manner of death seals his failure and victimhood.[14] Bakhtinian analysis suggests that efforts to make cosmic or general evaluations of the fall, or even specific assessments from very diverse contexts, miss the point of answerability. The death of Saul has to be read in terms of the life we have seen him live. The king falls in a brief moment of answerability. Discussions of how the Israelites (or others since) look upon suicide are out of place here. In this representation of the collapse and end of Saul's reign, and insofar as his reign is a paradigm for that of all other kings, Saul acts decisively "under his own signature," something he has failed to do throughout. As late as the night before his death we heard him tell Samuel that he had him raised from the dead "so that you will tell me what to do"; Samuel can tell him that his death will be on the morrow and in a battle with the Philistines. But Samuel cannot tell Saul how to die. Nor, so far as we can see, does God help Saul with that. Long silent, God seems to offer no opening to Saul at the end; or at least there is no evidence of it except in the gracious gift of his final meal. Whether and how Saul is strengthened by his last meal is a reader's call. Before moving on to the multiple and immediate reactions to the tragedy of Gilboa the narrator concludes this long monarchic event globally. When the news was heard, many beyond the Jezreel Valley and the Jordan fled their heritage toward the east, and, the narrator concludes, the Philistines came and occupied those places. Many are swept away into exile as the king falls in battle.

Contested reception of Saul's death
(1 Samuel 31:8–2 Samuel 1:27)

Though he has just provided a long "flashforward" on the outcome of the event—Israel dead or dispersed into exile—the narrator now provides four nearer views of Saul's fall, two pairs. The first pair diverges radically

---

[14] Among recent biblical commentators David M. Gunn, *The Fate of King Saul: An Interpretation of a Biblical Story* (Sheffield: JSOT Press, 1980) 111–12 assesses that the death comes with dignity, avoiding further humiliation; Edelman, *Saul* 284, sees it as a final attempt to thwart God's will. Fokkelman is of the opinion that Saul falls from the high place to the depths, harassed by God for reasons that are not wholly explicable. Saul resisted an unacceptable destiny and bows to his fate only at the end, a victim of God (*Fates* 691).

(31:8-13). The Philistines construe the death of Saul as a matter of great rejoicing for their people and their gods. Finding Saul's body the next day, they strip and dishonor it, sending his armor to adorn and honor the shrines of gods who rival Yʜwʜ, Saul's beheaded corpse to rejoice the citizens of Beth-Shan. Both gods and citizens of Israel's foes rejoice at the royal death. It is a tribute to Saul as well as a defilement. But the people of Jabesh Gilead, whom Saul had served well in their time of need (ch. 11), immediately contest that interpretation and travel by night, urgently and secretly we may suppose, to remove the bodies of Saul and his sons from Philistine walls and to burn them and then bury the remains under a tamarisk tree at Jabesh (31:11-13). They thus cancel out the Philistine viewpoint of rejoicing with a period of fasting. This interpretation also and more directly credits Saul.

The second pair of constructions of the king's death (2 Sam 1:1-27), also continuing to debate the honor-dishonor question, is more complex and requires slightly more attention from us. First comes the report of an Amalekite to David. Scholarly attention has moved from working to resolve the obvious differences between his account and that of chapter 31 (by adducing multiple sources) to sorting the ambiguity issues in terms of literary theory and reading strategies. Though it is valid, indeed crucial, to examine the responses of David, what I wish to maintain focus upon here is the question of how the mighty have fallen, how the king will be seen and said to have died. And given my supposition that Saul—whether living or dead—represents in some way the experience of monarchy in Israel and prompts a riddle for negotiation, we need to understand what the question is as well as the answer. So we have here a pair of alternate representations, first a sideshadow of what must not be allowed to stand, thrusting its way to take a position beside the more acceptable version of events.

The Amalekite offers a scenario that resembles closely what we have just seen, in fact chronologically overlapping it. David is slaying Amalekites as Philistines kill Saul, though David allows four hundred of them to escape, with the result that one turns up at Gilboa. This messenger's recital also rings powerfully the topos of 1 Samuel 4:12-18, where a lone Benjamin runner comes to tell the story of the fall of Eli's sons to their father, who joins them in death upon hearing of it. Contrary to Eli, who did not question the witness, David here asks the man how he knows that the king is dead. The story that issues from the man's lips in response to David's prompting draws a scene far more ignominious for the king than the one we heard Saul dread. The refugeeing Amalekite reports himself (understandably) undistracted by the taboo against the killing of the king, rather prompted purely by practical matters. The king will die in any case, and

the Amalekite is able to harvest a gain from it for himself, for David, perhaps for others. The man's recital maintains that Saul knew the identity of
the man he asked to help him exit his life. Being killed by a survivor of
Amalekites, the group Saul refused to extirpate and that David failed to
capture as well, seems far more shameful, it seems to me, than Saul's dying
at the hands of Philistine archers. The Amalekite's story—which David
almost chokes off by executing him—manages, if discredited, to whisper
that kingship ends because of the refusal of the kings to execute their
ancient and dread foes. Saul is once again made complicit —though not
answerable—for his own deeds.

David attempts to render the version of Amalekite agency both un-
thinkable and unrewardable, countering it with his own most memorable
response to the death of Saul and his dynasty (2 Sam 1:17-27). Like Hannah's
song, the complex poetry of David's eulogy demands more attention than
space provides here. It continues to be for me one of the most beautiful
texts in the Hebrew Bible. But as I scan it here for its contribution to the
question of the manner of Saul's death I find it strangely muted. Besides its
clearest denial—that one of the Amalekites whom Saul and David allowed
to escape is the one who brings down the king—its subtler double-voicing
visits many sites both in our story of Saul and beyond.[15] How does David
represent the death of Saul? As in the case of the Amalekite narrative, I will
focus on the question of the manner of the king's falling rather than on the
sincerity of the reciting voice. David here not so much rebuts as rises above
the ignominious construction of the Amalekite to draw a more honorable
picture. David opens with a lament for the glory of Israel, lying slain on the
high place. The mighty fallen is a glory in just what way? As the eulogy
draws its hero, David balances the rejoicing of Philistine women with the
lament of Israelite women. Granted the difficulty of choosing how to praise
a fallen opponent, after David lauds the valiant though clearly ineffective
valor of Saul and Jonathan his other choices seem strained. The grief for
Saul is pictured through the eyes of those for whom he provided luxury, an
achievement of Saul we have not heard previously. David's praise of
Jonathan likewise omits (understandably) to praise a friend for his long
support of David and focuses instead on David's appreciation of Jonathan's
love for him, granted the word may imply political loyalty as well as personal love. The royal shield, lying begrimed and unoiled amid the carnage,
is in some ways the most poignant image.

---

[15] Those interested in the rich detail might consult the various commentaries already in
service in this book.

Conclusions

Though we are about to review this long reading of Saul, a brief summary is in order here. As we shifted away from our last set of biblical material into this concluding set (from Chapter 7 to Chapter 8 of the present book), we had witnessed a honing of the question of the king's death. The clearest statement was that no Israelite could, without blame, raise a hand to harm God's anointed. We had heard David speculate about how Saul might die: at God's hands, naturally in the course of things, by Philistine agency. We had seen little indication that Saul would terminate his kingship himself. Our present material has taken care to remove David from the scene so that it cannot be supposed that he was on Gilboa when kingship fell. The Philistines are surely in evidence there, and in a general sense it becomes clear that Saul dies not simply in the course of a life but while fighting that dread enemy. The two possibilities remaining from David's prior ruminations and from the narrator's general portrait of Saul received further development.

As we saw, when his moment comes Saul himself performs the deed that terminates his monarchy and his life: he falls upon his own sword, though not without first having asked another to help him avoid such a choice. Answerability does not come easy to Saul. His death, and that of his sons, is definitive; a sprig from Saul's stock will appear just beyond the bend in this winding story but fail to take root. Leadership, the care for the "one thing needful," will pass elsewhere. Saul has, on the night before his death, been sufficiently lost as to reach out to the outlawed and the dead for help. Saul could hear nothing from God, nothing from prophet or priest, and so illicit access to the realm of the divine becomes his choice. What he learns there is not pleasing, but perhaps is crucial for him. What becomes undeniable even by Saul is that God is the one Saul has been opposing in his dealings with David. Hardly news to us, it is arguably a great insight for Saul, one he can take in finally in his nonroyal (dis)guise. How, you may ask, does Saul cope with information that has been fruitlessly tapping him on the shoulder for lo these many pages? Saul is good at asking, better at denying, best at refusing to answer for what is his own doing. How is it credible that he makes a shift here?

Bound in with this question of Saul's asking and answering is the mystery of God's communication, self-disclosure. How does God commune with us? How do *you* assume, understand it to occur? Our story has made it clear that (unlike David in ch. 23, for example) Saul never registers experience of a subject-to-subject utterance from God. Utterances, at least in the sense that Bakhtin has developed, are shaped by both parties involved. God cannot "send" one to a person unable or unwilling to receive it; that is, God cannot shape an utterance with a refusing party. As Saul has reduced himself to being king he has put himself at fundamental odds with God, who sees someone else in that role, and presumably sees Saul in some other guise. When Saul, for whatever motives and responding to whatever prompt, adopts such a dis-guise for himself, he moves closer into mutual utterance construction with God. Though most of what Saul learns while in the medium's presence seems frightening and unwelcome to him, its bluntness about times and places appears to penetrate. When the raised-up Samuel says that Saul will be joining his dead prophet tomorrow, surely Saul's urgency is sharpened. If I am right to think that the identity of his adversary comes as fresh news, my sense is that such insight arrives with a jolt as well. His last help comes "from another quarter":[16] a woman urges him to eat and prepares his last meal for him. Strengthened by her gesture, Saul moves on to sign his life as he hands it over. The moment of empathy, which is the place of shared experience from which the woman reads her visitor—who had both declared her illegal and then asked her to intercede for him with the invisible powerful ones—breaks through Saul's isolation and unrelatedness. It changes little about his life except the manner of his leaving it. Saul dies well.

---

[16] The expression is used to Queen Esther by her cousin Mordecai when he is trying to persuade her to use her position to assist the threatened Jews (Esth 4:14).

CONCLUSION

What have we done in our reading of this biblical story? How have we arrived at this particular portrait of King Saul? Let me review my sense of our process while inviting you to do the same. Perhaps the most fundamental thing we have done is to ask questions. When my friends asked me why I was spending so much time on Saul their question pushed me to realize that I was first drawn to Saul because he talked to himself. He seemed a character worth coming to know. And so I began to pose my questions to the text and to other scholars who had worked with 1 Samuel. The reading strategies of Mikhail Bakhtin, surely complex but insistent on the importance of our intense engagement with the narrative, have helped me read better: you too, I hope. Bakhtin's insistence upon dialogue in its many forms, on the need for our active partnership in constructing our language and our worlds of meaning have, I hope, opened the biblical text to many more possibilities than you sensed were available when we started this project.

You brought questions as well, perhaps found others as we went along. I cannot know all of them, though I can guess at some. The point is that you and those with whom you have been reading have been enriched, your imaginations activated by all of the questions in circulation. The INTERFACES series is constructed so as to prompt such links, endlessly. In this book I wagered for us that the writer of 1 Samuel was asking his king to do two things. First, Saul must serve as the embodiment of Israel's whole experience with kings. It is not easy for a character to embody something so longitudinally complex. I may be wrong about my hunch that Saul was crafted to serve as a riddle about kingship, that the story was shaped for a sixth-century community with its own leadership problem: How to return from exile? If—or since—not with kings, why not, and how not? Why was monarchy a failure-not-to-be-repeated, and how can such a venerable institution come to a legitimate and morally healthy close? But stories work contextually and not simply abstractly, and my hypothesis about an original situation for this one continues to strike me as plausible. Easier, I suspect, was the second task our storyteller assigned his main character. Saul is drawn as a human being who shows us many facets of how relationships work: with our friends, our foes, our families, and with God. In any case, proposing these purposes helps us engage more actively as we read, if only to resist sliding along with what we have already thought and to expose possibilities that need deepening.

The early part of the story (the first seven chapters of 1 Samuel) showed us, at least in our present interpretation, a sort of dress rehearsal for the story of Saul. We first saw a set of characters, related but somewhat at cross-purposes, asking for a son, whose name made a wordplay on that very verb: Saul as a request and a bequest. The asked-for son arrived, but to what end was not so clear. In a next section that seemed to trace in miniature Israel's larger story of exile we watched the ark of the covenant journey into a foreign land and then return again, with leadership uncertain. If you entertained my hypothesis, that the ark was a tangible representation of the relationship between God and Israel, then it was not so difficult to see the ark's adventures as rehearsing God and Israel's sixth-century exile to Babylon. If the riddle works as I propose, the ark's troubled return made clear the urgency for new leadership. The care of the ark, of the bond uniting people and deity, was not to be entrusted to the old Elide dynasty who mistreated it, or even to the care of Samuel. Who would be called forth for this task of fresh leadership?

The third section of our reading, resembling in a sense the first three chapters of 1 Samuel, showed a set of diverse people asking for a king. They were sure that they wanted a king, and in time most were sure that Saul was to be the king. Not so much the request itself but the manner of making it was flawed, since God appears not to have been thought of, let alone asked anything by the elders. God had certain reservations about the project but certainly participated in the naming of the king. God's prophet Samuel, whatever else he may have neglected to communicate to the people, made it clear that king and people had one primary thing to do, "one thing needful," which was to deepen the relationship between God and Israel. The Bible in general, and surely 1 Samuel and its Deuteronomistic matrix, maintains that working at that relationship is primary for God and needs to be urgent for us as well, challenging though it often seems. Saul himself posed certain questions about his kingship, starting with "why me?" But though starting reluctant, he seemed quickly to define himself in terms of being king. As we watched, it became clear that Saul was perhaps unwilling and surely unable to do the one thing needful. It is important to remember that, if I am correct in my wager that Saul is a cipher for a several-hundred-year experience of Israel with kings, his representation has to be *that* he failed. In other words, the Saul storyteller is not giving us a factual report on what went wrong historically, but making an experience visible for us to see and ponder helpfully. Concentrically, first the son of Hannah, then those of Eli and Samuel, and next the sons of Saul—David's too, if you keep reading—made clear why sons, kings, were an inadequate resolution to the problem of leadership. But to make the point sharp our bard sketched Saul on two occasions unable to manage well the mix of military and cultic matters, crucial for the health of the God-Israel relationship. Historians could add other socio-economic reasons as well to illustrate that kings were, overall, harmful to common life. And not only did Saul fail: He refused to own his failure, to shoulder it, to learn from it. He blamed the others and denied his own responsibility. And so God fired Saul from this job that most crucially needed doing and that Saul was shown unable to do. If you have issues of fairness with God they probably surfaced here. The relationship between the king and the deity, between Saul and YHWH, offers us ready if sometimes painful access to the mystery of how God does with us, how we do with God. Saul gives every appearance of doing poorly; God as well, you may feel. The story's gift is that certain parts of the struggle we all feel with God at one time or another are presented to us here for our reflection, our negotiation.

For the story of Saul moves on to explore in the detail of his human relationships where Saul seemed to go awry. As we listened to a troubled king invite the young shepherd from Bethlehem into his household to soothe his ravings, as we watched Saul offer that young man his own royal armor to fight the giant whom the king feared to engage, I suspect we felt for Saul. As David grew in popularity, Saul came to resent it. But Saul's efforts to thwart David seemed to twist out of his control and boomerang on the old king. Saul's object of dread—the possibility that he might not be king—was ironically made all the more likely by his way of dealing with David and others. The court buzzed with discourse; Saul talked to himself. Saul used his household—his own children—to get at David, and they seemed to Saul, perhaps to us, to choose David over against their father and king. Saul's desires, his choices, were shown conflicted. A man at war with himself, Saul was unable to mind carefully the relationship holding God and people together. As the story moved on, Saul alienated his prophet, the priests, his own kin in the Benjamin tribe, whom he accused of taking bribes. Saul, for all practical purposes, chased David from his palace—having invited him to come—and then began the all-consuming task of pursuing him.

If the story of Saul had shown the incapacity of the "old sons" to rule well, had shown how and why they governed badly, it moved next to deal with the question of how the *ancien regime* was to be replaced. As Saul tracked David it became apparent soon enough that David was the more skilled hunter and that Saul became David's quarry. Having started with the hint that David was in danger from Saul, we saw it more likely that David would kill Saul. And yet the story is very insistent that, though tempted, David resists occasions to do that. No member of the community, surely not the most obvious rival, was to raise a hand to bring the monarchy down. Such attempts, visible frequently in the long story of kings that unfolds after Saul (and that he epitomizes), are morally polluting and politically destructive. However monarchy will end, it will not be done violently and by the hand of its replacement. If David rehearsed the possibility that God would dispatch Saul, that did not happen either. The inverse of God's ignoring Saul involves a certain permissiveness. Our storyteller toyed with a scenario in which God struck the isolated old man, but it was a fantasy, rehearsing mainly to deny. We may have supposed that the Philistines would kill Saul, and indeed it is his last articulated fear. But on the night before he died Saul had some sort of experience that shifted something in him. What it was remains for us to puzzle out. He learned from Samuel that he and his sons would die the next day. Saul seems finally to have taken in that his opponent all the while had not been so much David but God. Saul had spent his life at cross-purposes with God. We may wonder that he did not know that, but our window is a bit different from his own. And additionally, Saul was the recipient of an act of kindness from a woman who strengthened him, braced his courage, gave him a sustaining meal.

So as he watched his sons die and saw the Philistines approach him he asked, begged his armor-bearer to kill him, but the young man refused. Thus in the end, with no one to blame or to shelter behind, Saul managed his own exit from the scene, bringing to an end his own tortured rule, symbolically drawing the curtain on Israel's monarchy. The riddle of Saul has indicated that the termination of the monarchy rested in the king's own hand. Though it is unlikely that we will ever know actual details about the termination of the Davidic monarchy in the late sixth century, my guess is that they would center in some determined and determining deed of the old royal survivor, Jehoiachin himself. Saul's death, in riddle terms, was not about an individual's suicide but pointed to the self-destructiveness and self-destroying nature of the royal institution. The riddle propounded the need for the crowned incumbent to manage the termination of the institution, and indeed, fragmentary though the trail is as the exile community returned, there was no crowned king for many generations to come. Saul's clearest and cleanest act, his least debated and retracted deed, was his answerability in bringing his own kingship down. It had been moribund for some time already; he simply terminated it decisively.

What is the gain from reading such a story, from reading this story as we have read it? The classics—like this one—work because over their long lives, they reach us in the places where we ponder our deepest questions. Their primary value is not in their historicity but in the skill behind their representation. As I have tried to demonstrate, the portrait does not root most deeply in realism, but there is a good deal in this drawing that I, for one, recognize, and I suspect you do as well. To create a distinctive and credible human being, especially one struggling so deeply in unrelation to self and all around him, is to pose an enigma or conundrum. It is in the verbal detail—particularly in character dialogues—that the human Saul emerges from the pages. Insofar as the sketch is good, key facets of our human experience resonate with it, even if we are at a substantial remove from the character in terms of the usual markers of race, gender, culture, class, religion, and caste. Saul, I think, is a well-drawn character, whose lineaments offer access to a human being swamped by terrible isolation and a consequent/contributory incapacity to act with integrity, answerability. Our last question in this particular reading is to speculate very briefly on how such a classic can work for us. Why do we read these stories, and with what effect? Let me suppose as well—not instead of but additionally—that the classic is the Bible. If it is the case for you as it is for me that the Bible is one of the most privileged places of God's self-disclosure, then we have a value-added classic. Though we struggle for the language to express it, many Jews and Christians through the centuries recognize and acknowledge that the biblical stories bring out in a particularly deep way the depths of what it is to be human before God, not to mention in company with other humans and the rest of creation. Bakhtin's sense of language dynamics is again helpful: he talks of utterances, discourse between (or among) interlocutors where the shaping of language is constituted continuously by everything operative in the relationship. That is, the Bible is not a great Behistun Rock, a self-congratulatory inscription announced by its author to the universe for reading by any who pass by with sufficient expertise, "playing" whether anyone listens or not. God's self-disclosure is an utterance, which requests and counts on active and customized participation by all wishing to engage. It is our common engagement with this text, the vast communal dimension of our use of it over space and time, that keeps such a text a prime place to meet God. Its use in prayer and liturgy adds richness as well.

Saul's life may not seem the best place to graze for such communication, since there is more wrong than right between king and deity in this long story. No Christian writer I am aware of has made Saul a (proto)type of Jesus, and such is no longer seen as a respectful or productive way to read Hebrew Bible narratives. But the well-told story has depths that serve readily for transformative reading, that is, appropriation that draws me— and I hope others—into a closer relationship with God. The question here is specifically how. Let me propose one possibility. I will bring to bear, in company with my conviction that God is longing to communicate and be in friendship with creatures like me and you—and Saul—this reading mode of sudden, often rueful and regretful recognition. It comes in a flash of familiarity that is so quick it penetrates defenses almost before we can dash to shelter behind them. Biblical characters do it, which prompts the reader similarly. You may have had the opportunity to see old film clips of the U.S. Civil Rights Movement (or similar events). On occasion the camera will have zoomed in at a demonstration (e.g., the one in Birmingham where the police used dogs and the protesters included children, the Memphis lunch counter sit-ins, or the march through a white suburb of Chicago) to show the opponents of the demonstrators. As I observe a Birmingham policeman allowing a German Shepherd to savage a child, watch the glee with which a white patron pours catsup and mustard over the head of an African American who is calmly awaiting service, or see a sneering blonde woman proudly waving signs she has inscribed with ugly and racist words, I wonder how they feel years later when they see themselves. I think I do not feel smug or righteous, since though I have not done quite those things, the portraits remind me of my own failed efforts to love a neighbor whole-heartedly. What I am after is the spot of imaginative, courageous, and empathetic recognition where the policeman might say that no matter what the provocation, he is shamed by the dogs; where the former lunch-counter patron can decide that the inhumanity of ridiculing and demeaning another is too high a price to pay for a whites-only lunch; where the woman concludes that whatever else might pertain, she does not want to own or invest further in the picture of herself so hating another. Another way to put that same dynamic is that I, catching sight of myself in the mirrors of those clips, can say either, "Not me, I've never done, would never do that," or may alternatively recognize myself, "Too close for comfort, I need to take care." The story of Saul can work in the second way, or does for me. The human enigma of Saul is his lack of capacity to be an answerable self in relation with others, especially God, who at best is challenging. It is that Saul I now want to read a final time. Since the character himself does not go reflective, I will perform that move from my own reader's point of view.

There are many "clips" in the story for us, more than for Saul, I think. We may move into the space he opens with his selftalk, those private ruminations he shares in our hearing. That he resists deeper insight does not mean we may not stand on his tall shoulders to see something of our own divided desires. Saul has had several occasions where he might have to-taled the list of what he was spending to get what he wanted. He seems to have looked the other way. But, if you follow my reading, on the night be-fore he died he recognized two "photographs": the first was handed Saul by his irascible prophet. It showed Saul locked in mortal combat with God, who regretted their struggle deeply. And the spirit-familiar showed him something gentler: a man she was willing to feed for his final struggle. If we are willing to ask our own questions boldly, to wager our self-knowledge as we work with the portrait called Saul, we are very likely to grow in self-knowledge, in insight, perhaps in wisdom. In the story there is no direct articulation of these things. The storyteller does not make it easy for us. It is, beyond a doubt, my own experience of God as shaped by the gospels that prompts me to construct this interaction on the basis of what Saul un-expectedly achieves. That is, the relationship with God made available specifically in the context of Jesus' life affects my reading of YHWH in the story of Saul. The gift offered Saul by the wise woman surely does not change his life completely. When his moment of death comes, as Samuel has promised him it was soon to do, Saul meets it slant as usual, hoping, asking that someone would do for him what he wished to avoid. But, that failing, he does it himself. How one leaves life signifies in biblical texts. My construction is that Saul's gift from the hand of the medium offers a moment of reconciliation with God, an opportunity to hear God's voice not simply from the scolding Samuel but also from the bracing witch who gave him the strength needed for his final and answerable deed. I grant it is apophatic, but that suits the story. God and Saul will no go all cuddly at the end. Saul does not die crying out for God. But insofar as he has allowed, perhaps even received gratefully the woman's portrait of him as cared-for and her gift of bread and meat, he shows us something about the one thing needful: the relationship with God.

BIBLIOGRAPHY

Ackerman, James S. "Who Can Stand before YHWH, This Holy God? A Reading of 1 Samuel 1–15," *Prooftexts* 11 (1991) 1–24.

Alter, Robert. *The David Story: A Translation with Commentary of 1 and 2 Samuel.* New York: W. W. Norton & Company, 1999.

Bach, Alice. *Women, Seduction, and Betrayal in Biblical Narrative.* Cambridge: Cambridge University Press, 1997.

Bakhtin, Mikhail. *The Dialogic Imagination: Four Essays.* Edited by Michael Holquist; translated by Caryl Emerson and Michael Holquist. Austin: University of Texas Press, 1981.

_____. *Problems of Dostoevsky's Poetics.* Edited and translated by Caryl Emerson. Minneapolis: University of Minnesota Press, 1984.

_____. *Speech Genres and Other Late Essays.* Edited by Caryl Emerson and Michael Holquist; translated by Vern W. McGee. Austin: University of Texas Press, 1986.

_____. "Author and Hero in Aesthetic Activity," in *Art and Answerability: Early Philosophical Essays by M. M. Bakhtin.* Edited by Michael Holquist and Vadim Liapunov; translated by Vadim Liapunov. Austin: University of Texas Press, 1990.

_____. *Toward a Philosophy of the Act.* Edited by Vadim Liapunov and Michael Holquist; translated by Vadim Liapunov. Austin: University of Texas Press, 1993.

Bakhtin, Mikhail, and V. N. Voloshinov. *Marxism and the Philosophy of Language.* Translated by Ladislav Matejka and I. R. Titunik. Cambridge, Mass.: Harvard University Press, 1973.

Bar Efrat, Shimon. *Narrative Art in the Bible.* Sheffield: Almond Press, 1989.

Berlin, Adele. *Poetics and Interpretation of Biblical Narrative.* Sheffield: Almond Press, 1983.

Beuken, W. A. M. "I Samuel 28: The Prophet as 'Hammer of Witches,'" *Journal for the Study of the Old Testament* 6 (1978) 3–17.

Campbell, Antony F., and Mark A. O'Brien. *Unfolding the Deuteronomistic History: Origins, Upgrades, Present Text.* Minneapolis: Fortress, 2000.

Clark, Katerina, and Michael Holquist. *Mikhail Bakhtin.* Cambridge: Harvard University Press, 1984.

Clines, David, and Tamara C. Eskenazi, eds. *Telling Queen Michal's Story: An Experiment in Comparative Interpretation.* Sheffield: JSOT Press, 1991.

Coggins, Richard. "On Kings and Disguises," *Journal for the Study of the Old Testament* 50 (1991) 55–62.

Craig, Kenneth M., Jr. "Rhetorical Aspects of Questions Answered with Silence in 1 Samuel 14:37 and 28:6," *Catholic Biblical Quarterly* 56 (1994) 221–39.

Dällenbach, Lucien. *The Mirror in the Text*. Translated by Jeremy Whiteley with Emma Hughes. Cambridge: Polity Press, 1989.

Dothan, Trude, and Moshe Dothan. *People of the Sea: The Search for the Philistines*. New York: Macmillan, 1992.

Edelman, Diana V. *King Saul in the Historiography of Judah*. Sheffield: Sheffield Academic Press, 1991.

Edelman, Diana. "Did Saulide-Davidic Rivalry Resurface in Early Persian Yehud?" in M. P. Graham and J. A. Dearman, eds., *The Land That I Will Show You: Essays in the History and Archaeology of the Ancient Near East in Honor of J. Maxwell Miller*. JSOTSup 343. Sheffield: Sheffield Academic Press, 2001, 70–92.

Esler, Philip. "The Madness of Saul: A Cultural Reading of 1 Samuel 8-31," in J. Cheryl Exum and Stephen D. Moore, eds., *Biblical Studies/Cultural Studies*. Sheffield: Sheffield Academic Press, 1998.

Eskenazi, Tamara Cohn. *In An Age of Prose: A Literary Approach to Ezra and Nehemiah*. Atlanta: Scholars, 1988.

Eslinger, Lyle. *Kingship of God in Crisis: A Close Reading of 1 Samuel 1–12*. Sheffield: Sheffield Academic Press, 1985.

Exum, J. Cheryl. *Tragedy and Biblical Narrative: Arrows of the Almighty*. Sheffield: Sheffield Academic Press, 1992.

Fokkelman, Jan P. *Narrative Art and Poetry in the Books of Samuel: Volume II: The Crossing Fates*. Assen, The Netherlands: Van Gorcum, 1986.

_____. *Narrative Art and Poetry in the Books of Samuel: Volume IV: Vow and Desire*. Assen, The Netherlands: Van Gorcum, 1993.

Fox, Everett. *Give Us A King! Samuel, Saul and David*. New York: Schocken, 1999.

Green, Barbara. *Mikhail Bakhtin and Biblical Scholarship: An Introduction*. Atlanta: Society of Biblical Literature Press, 2000.

_____. "The Engaging Nuances of Genre: Reading Saul and Michal Afresh," in Carleen Mandolfo and Timothy Sandoval, eds., *Relating to the Text: Form-Critical and Interdisciplinary Insights Into the Bible*. Sheffield: Sheffield Academic Press, forthcoming.

_____. *How Are the Mighty Fallen? A Dialogical Study of Saul in 1 Samuel*. Sheffield: Sheffield Academic Press, forthcoming.

Gunn, David M. *The Fate of King Saul: An Interpretation of a Biblical Story*. Sheffield: JSOT Press, 1980.

Japhet, Sara. "Sheshbazzar and Zerubbabel: Against the Background of the Historical and Religious Tendencies of Ezra-Nehemiah. *Zeitschrift für die Alttestamentliche Wissenshaft* 95 (1983) 218–29.

Jobling, David. *1 Samuel*. Berit Olam: Studies in Hebrew Narrative and Poetry. Collegeville: The Liturgical Press, 1998.

Klein, Ralph W. *1 Samuel*. Waco: Word Books, 1983.

McCarter, P. Kyle. *1 Samuel. A New Translation with Introduction and Commentary*. Garden City, N. Y.: Doubleday, 1980.

Miscall, Peter D. *1 Samuel: A Literary Reading*. Bloomington: Indiana University Press, 1986.

Morson, Gary S. *Narrative Freedom and the Shadows of Time*. New Haven: Yale University Press, 1994.

Nelson, Richard D. *Joshua: A Commentary*. Louisville: Westminster John Knox, 1997.

Newsom, Carol A. "Bakhtin," in A.K.M. Adam, ed., *Handbook of Postmodern Biblical Interpretation*. St. Louis: Chalice Press, 2000.

Polzin, Robert M. *Samuel and the Deuteronomist: A Literary Study of the Deuteronomic History: 1 Samuel*. San Francisco: Harper & Row, 1989.

Pyper, Hugh S. *David as Reader: 2 Samuel 12:1-15 and the Poetics of Fatherhood*. Leiden: E. J. Brill, 1996.

Reis, Pamela Tamarkin. "Eating the Blood: Saul and the Witch of Endor," *Journal for the Study of the Old Testament* 73 (1997) 3–23.

Schneiders, Sandra M. "The Study of Christian Spirituality: Contours and Dynamics of a Discipline," *Christian Spirituality Bulletin* 6/1 (1998) 1, 3–12.

Seow, C. L. "Ark of the Covenant," *Anchor Bible Dictionary*. David Noel Freedman, ed. New York: Doubleday, 1992, 1:386–93.

Understanding Scripture through the characters of the Bible

interfaces

Students will learn appropriate tools of inquiry and interpretation

Barbara Green, O.P., Editor

Interfaces is a curriculum adventure and a creative opportunity in teaching and learning. Each volume focuses on a biblical character or a pair of them. The characters are in some cases powerful and familiar, though in other cases they are minor and little-known. Each author uses one or more study methods to examine how a character interfaces with his or her historical-cultural world and other characters. In the process you will learn how to read the Bible with critical insight.

Rights: World, English

For more information about
the *Interfaces* series
visit www.litpress.org
or call 1.800.858.5450

LITURGICAL PRESS

St. John's Abbey, Collegeville, MN 56321-7500